CLASSIC COCKTAILS

DONE WELL

CLASSIC COCKTAILS

DONE WELL

TRIED-AND-TRUE RECIPES
for the HOME BARTENDER

FAITH HINGEY

PHOTOGRAPHY BY CLARE BARBOZA

Zeitgeist • New York

CONTENTS

INTRODUCTION

Going out for cocktails with friends and family is one of my favorite things to do, but I believe these boozy delights are just as enjoyable in the comfort of your own home. My cocktail-making journey began years ago with cheap liquor, plastic-bottled citrus juices, and lots of Coke and Sprite. When I started stocking my home bar, I found myself overwhelmed and confused trying to figure out what to buy. I wanted ingredients that were versatile enough to make a wide variety of drinks while staying within my limited budget and space. I didn't know what to do with the bottles I accumulated, and I was constantly missing ingredients for the interesting cocktails I wanted to make. Every trip to the liquor store felt like playing roulette—which bottle would finally be *the one*?

I was determined to learn, so I began researching and teaching myself the classics. In 2017, I started documenting my cocktail journey online (@barfaith on Instagram; barfaith.com). My goal was to share everything I learned to make home bartending a little less intimidating for others. Now I'm excited to share my tried-and-true tips and classic, well-loved recipes. Whether you're new to home bartending or you've already got a sizable bar, this book will guide you in curating a collection that's focused yet versatile.

My cocktail interests have always been strongly influenced by the classics, so in these pages, you'll find recipes for 75 classic cocktails that will turn your home into a craft cocktail bar. Soon you'll experience the joys of having the perfect cocktail in hand, whether it's sipping on an Old Fashioned with a home-cooked meal, delivering bottomless pours of French 75s while hosting brunch with friends, curling up on the couch with a hot Apple Toddy in your favorite mug, or entertaining guests with a sophisticated cocktail night, complete with Martinis, Manhattans, and Margaritas. Cheers!

CHAPTER ONE

THE CLASSICS AT HOME

You're likely no stranger to pouring a glass of wine for dinner or popping open a cold beer for a summer barbecue. But perhaps you've always wanted to whip up a Negroni to go with your pasta dinner or serve icy Mint Juleps on a hot afternoon. Learning to make your favorite classic cocktails at home will allow you to elevate just about any activity, whether it's movie night with your partner, brunch with friends, or just you and a good book on a lazy evening. The tips and tricks you'll learn in this chapter will have you shaking, stirring, and sipping in style in no time.

STUDYING THE CLASSICS

Classic cocktails provide a window into the past. Consider the underground bar, the hidden bar behind a rotating bookshelf, or the windowless bar decked out in nautical adornments. These charming places provide a glimpse of life in another era, where drinking a storied libation is really a form of time travel.

The modern cocktail library remains deeply rooted in historical drinks. Studying classic recipes provides us with fundamental knowledge for informed experimentations with modern ingredients and styles. Each cocktail has its own stories to tell, and as you learn them, you'll observe trends that evolved alongside historical events.

Early American settlers had limited access to European spirits; therefore, many early cocktail recipes included spirits from common crops grown in the New World, such as corn (bourbon) and apples (apple brandy).

During American Prohibition, many skilled bartenders left to work in other countries. Their ideas and recipes spread globally, and likewise, they discovered new ingredients that would later be introduced to the American cocktail scene. In the United States, the limited availability of liquor—much of which was tampered with or of questionable origin—encouraged people to go to great efforts to mask the vile pungency of these spirits. The challenges of this era resulted in notable flavor innovation.

By the mid-1900s, the advent of commercial air travel and American soldiers returning from World War II led to the introduction of new spirits and ideas from around the world, including rums from the Caribbean, vodka from Russia, and imagery and flavors inspired by Polynesia (though it is important to note the décor associated with

American tiki bars is not accurate and generalizes the cultures and peoples of the Pacific Islands).

The latter half of the twentieth century saw the emergence of new artificial flavors, thickeners, and bright colors. While interesting, these ingredients didn't make for the best cocktails. Known as the cocktail Dark Ages, this era was marked by radioactive-colored drinks, fake fruit flavorings, and overly sweet drinks.

Enter the cocktail revival of the twenty-first century. Many of the drinks served today are strongly inspired by the same classics enjoyed by generations past—those that were truly worth rediscovering.

Cocktail Styles

As you explore, you'll find recurring patterns in the composition of classic cocktails—these can be considered cocktail archetypes. Using these archetypes as inspiration, you can confidently design new drinks by substituting one or two ingredients with something similar; for example, replace lemon juice with lime juice, simple syrup with a different sweetener, or brandy with whiskey. Here are some classic styles that recur throughout both historic and modern cocktails:

APERITIVO. In Italian tradition, diners often enjoy aperitivo cocktails before meals. These lighter, often bubbly drinks made with bittersweet liqueurs stimulate the appetite. The Americano (page 159) and Negroni Sbagliato (page 174) are examples of fizzy versions, while the Negroni (page 65), Boulevardier (page 76), and Rosita (page 177) represent slightly heavier options.

BUCK. The buck is a simple drink primarily composed of a spirit, citrus juice, and ginger beer. This drink works with all sorts of spirits, including gin, bourbon, rum, and Tequila. The type of citrus used will change the balance of the drink; different combinations include the Gin Buck (page 53) and Moscow Mule (page 173).

PUNCH. Punch is one of the oldest forms of a mixed alcoholic drink. Earliest references date to the 1600s, and one theory is that the name originates from the Hindi word for five, *panch*, for its five primary ingredients: alcohol, citrus, sugar, water, and spice. Punch bowls were shared by America's founding fathers to celebrate the signing of the Declaration of Independence, British Royal Navy sailors on early colonizing expeditions, and all rungs of society gathering to socialize, gossip, and conspire. From a classic Brandy Punch (page 118) to the Carribbean Rum Punch (page 155), the potential combinations of these festive bowls are endless.

SLING. One of the oldest and most rudimentary ways to enhance a spirit, slings are made by adding water, a bit of sugar, and sometimes a spice, such as nutmeg. Examples include the Whiskey Sling (page 105), Bumbo (page 138), and Apple Toddy (page 110).

COCKTAIL. Before it became a generic term for all mixed drinks, the earliest form of a cocktail was nothing more than a spirit embellished with sugar, a bit of water, and bitters. The cocktail was an evolution of the sling archetype, swapping the spices for bitters. The whiskey-based cocktail is what we now refer to as the Old Fashioned, but this format of a core spirit with a bit of sweetener and aromatics also appears in drinks like the Sazerac (page 98), Mint Julep (page 93), and Manhattan (page 90).

SOURS. Consisting of a strong spirit balanced by tart and sweet elements, sours are usually shaken and can be served either in a coupe glass (a shallow stemmed glass) or in a rocks glass with ice. The Daiquiri (page 141), Whiskey Sour (page 107), Sidecar (page 129), and Lemon Drop (page 168) are a few classic examples. Sours are a very broad style, and several other archetypes are related to or are subtypes of the sour, such as the collins, fizz, and daisy.

COLLINS. This tall, fizzy drink dating back to the 1800s originally featured gin and lemon. The collins is essentially a sour that's served over ice with sparkling water to lengthen the drink for slower sipping. The Tom Collins (page 69) is one of the oldest surviving forms of the collins, so popular that it inspired the collins glass. Other examples following this general template include the Paloma (page 176), Mojito (page 149), and Long Island Iced Tea (page 170).

FIZZ. Like the collins, the fizz is a bubbly, sweet, and tart drink originally made with gin, lemon, and sparkling water. Fizzes are generally served without additional ice, making them a "shorter" drink that's meant to be imbibed more quickly than collins-style drinks. Beyond the basic Gin Fizz (page 56), classic ways to enhance a fizz include adding eggs or aromatics like mint or switching up the base spirit, like in the Brandy Fizz (page 115).

DAISY. The daisy is a style of sour that uses fruit liqueur and is usually served over ice. In the late 1800s, orange liqueur was the popular choice; 50 years later, it was displaced by grenadine. Examples of the daisy include the Gin Daisy (page 54), Rum Daisy (page 154), Knickerbocker (page 146), and Margarita (page 171).

FLIP. Historically very popular, flips are less common today. The key marker of a flip is the inclusion of a whole raw egg mixed into a base spirit and sugar. The emulsifying properties of the egg lead to a rich and creamy delight. Frequently served hot back in the day, they are now usually served cold. A great example is the Egg Flip (page 122), and with the addition of cream, you have Eggnog (page 124)!

A HOME BAR FOR THE AGES

Stocking a home bar can be overwhelming! That's why it makes sense to start with the classics. Many classic cocktails predate modern conveniences like artisanal syrups and craft liqueurs; as such, you'll need relatively few bottles to re-create them. The ingredients in this section are used repeatedly throughout the book and are essential to further your exploration into the world of cocktails.

The Classic Core Spirits

Most early cocktails were primarily made using American and European spirits such as whiskey, brandy, and gin, whereas spirits such as rum, Tequila, and vodka were latecomers in the American cocktail scene. These core spirits are the primary components upon which classic cocktails are built, so it's important to choose quality products. Many classic cocktails can be made by swapping base spirits, so one extra core spirit can notably expand the versatility of your bar. I recommend stocking at least one bottle of each kind.

AMERICAN WHISKEY (BOURBON AND RYE). Whiskey is made by fermenting and distilling grains, then aging it in wooden barrels. Unlike other styles of whiskey, American bourbon and rye whiskeys are always aged in *new* oak barrels, which results in very strong wood flavors. Bourbon is made with at least 51 percent corn and has strong notes of vanilla and caramel, whereas rye is made with at least 51 percent rye grain and has a spicier profile and therefore a stronger presence in cocktails. They are somewhat interchangeable, but swapping them will alter the overall characteristic of the drink. Bourbon tends to be more approachable for those less experienced with whiskey. Good choices of both include Buffalo Trace and Elijah Craig (bourbons) and Rittenhouse Rye.

IRISH WHISKEY. Irish whiskey, the leading style of whiskey in the world until the early twentieth century, is a common choice for pre-Prohibition drinks. It tends to be lighter, fruitier, and less woody and oak dominant than American whiskeys. Look for an Irish whiskey labeled Single Pot Still, such as Powers or Redbreast, to stay truer to historical styles and for a richer flavor.

COGNAC BRANDY. Any spirit made using fruit is considered a brandy, and Cognac is a French grape-based brandy especially popular in pre-Prohibition recipes. It's mellow, fruity, and almost caramel-like. Cognac has several label tiers based on how long it's been aged; a VS should be sufficient for cocktails, though a VSOP/Reserve may provide richer flavor. Try Rémy Martin.

APPLE BRANDY. Apple brandy is made from distilled and barrel-aged hard apple cider. While fruity and reminiscent of apple pie, apple brandy contains no sugar and is not sweet. Note that Applejack is not a pure apple brandy, as it is blended with a neutral grain spirit. I recommend a 100 percent pure apple brandy, such as Laird's Straight Apple Brandy, for a more concentrated flavor.

GIN. Gin is a crisp, herbal spirit with juniper as a primary flavor and numerous other botanicals for a bouquet of flavors. The London Dry gin variety is a good choice for recipes in this book, as it has a generally consistent flavor profile across brands. Tanqueray and Beefeater are good choices. Anything that's not London Dry can vary dramatically in flavor, because different producers express their creativity with all sorts of botanical combinations.

RUM. Rum is made using sugarcane juice or molasses. Like all distilled spirits, it contains no sugar after it's undergone this process. Rum can be divided into many subcategories and vary drastically in flavor. For the recipes in this book, look for a light rum that's clear with a mild flavor (The Real McCoy 3, El Dorado 3, Mount Gay Silver), a gold rum that's medium-bodied with some woodiness (Mount Gay Eclipse, The Real McCoy 5), and an aged gold rum with a rich, mellow flavor from longer aging in wood (Mount Gay XO, Real McCoy 12). Avoid spiced, flavored, and heavily darkened rums, as those have strong flavors that make them less versatile for classic cocktails.

TEQUILA. This grassy, herbaceous Mexican spirit is made by roasting, fermenting, and distilling the agave plant. Choose a Tequila that is 100 percent agave, as those without such labeling are usually mixed with a neutral grain spirit, which reduces the depth of flavor. Blanco (silver) Tequila is brighter in flavor, great for refreshing cocktails, while reposado (gold) is more mellow, for drinks with more spice or complexity. Try Cimarron, Cazadores, or Espolòn.

VODKA. This flavorless and odorless spirit is typically used when other flavors need to shine. Vodka can be made from anything, so long as it's distilled to 95 percent ABV (alcohol by volume), which removes most organic compounds that produce flavor. Before bottling, vodka is brought down to the common 40 percent ABV (alcohol by volume) by diluting with water. Any vodka would work; perhaps go with Ketel One or any locally produced vodka.

Liqueurs and Wines

Liqueurs and wines are as essential as core spirits for a balanced home bar. You only need a relatively small set to re-create a diverse variety of classic cocktails, and each of these is used repeatedly across recipes.

ORANGE LIQUEUR. These come in two main varieties: Curaçao and Triple Sec. Both are infused with orange peels; however, Curaçao generally has an aged brandy base, whereas Triple Sec has a neutral clear base. You can use these interchangeably, but opt for quality versions—some lesser varieties are artificially flavored or are sickeningly sweet. French products such as Cointreau, Pierre Ferrand Dry Curaçao, and Grand Marnier work best to re-create classic recipes.

BÉNÉDICTINE. This is a one-of-a-kind, centuries-old complex liqueur made with 27 herbs and spices—many of which are a closely guarded secret. It has strong notes of honey, baking spices, and citrus.

LUXARDO MARASCHINO LIQUEUR. Maraschino liqueur is made using sour cherries, including the pits. This clear liqueur is distinctive, medicinal, and nutty. A small 375-milliliter bottle will last you a long time since it's used in extremely small portions due to its potent flavor.

GREEN CHARTREUSE. This herbal liqueur is made by Carthusian monks using 130 secret herbs and spices. It's uniquely minty, herbaceous, vegetal, spiced, and citrusy—nothing matches its complex flavor.

CAMPARI. This red, bittersweet Italian liqueur is best known in the Negroni, but versatile in many appetite-stimulating libations.

ABSINTHE. Absinthe is made using anise, fennel, and wormwood. It adds a wonderful depth to cocktails and is typically used in very small quantities—often just a few drops. It's worth exploring, even if you're a bit shy when it comes to licorice. And contrary to rumors, absinthe is not hallucinogenic! Recommended brands include St. George Absinthe Verte and Vieux Pontarlier. You may find it helpful to transfer some into a small dropper bottle (available at health food stores or online). It's much easier to dispense a controlled amount from a dropper bottle than pouring directly from the liquor bottle.

SPARKLING WINE. Sparkling wine is produced using different methods that create variations in flavor and mouthfeel. Choose something you'd enjoy drinking on its own. Prosecco (produced in Italy) is fruity and has larger bubbles and works well for refreshing spritzer-like drinks, whereas Champagne (produced in France) and Cava (produced in Spain) have finer bubbles that complement more refined drinks.

SWEET/RED VERMOUTH. Sweet, or red (Rosso/Rouge/Rojo), vermouth is a fortified, aromatized wine, created by macerating and infusing wine with herbs, roots, and spices. A distilled spirit is added to increase its alcohol content to between 15 and 20 percent, and it's sweetened, making it rich and fragrant. Carpano Antica Formula, Cocchi Vermouth di Torino, and Dolin Rouge are good options. Once opened, it must be refrigerated and will keep for up to six months.

DRY VERMOUTH. Dry vermouth is also a fortified, aromatized wine. It's herbaceous and light, with minimal to no sweetness. Dry vermouth is different from white (Blanco/Blanc) vermouth; the latter is much sweeter. I recommend Dolin Dry or Noilly Prat Extra Dry. Once opened, dry vermouth must be refrigerated and will keep for up to two or three months.

Bitters

Bitters are a concentrated liquid extraction of herbs, spices, and aromatics. They bring *oomph* and unparalleled complexity to a drink. Dozens of bitters are available today, but these are the only three you'll need to re-create most classics:

ANGOSTURA AROMATIC BITTERS. With strong flavors of nutmeg, cloves, and baking spices, these are the single most important bitters for any home bar.

PEYCHAUD'S BITTERS. This bright red, anise-heavy, Creole-style bitter is a common ingredient in many classic New Orleans recipes.

REGANS' ORANGE BITTERS NO. 6. An aromatic, bitter ingredient that adds complexity and brightens the flavors in a drink.

Modifiers and Garnishes

Spirits and liqueurs may be the stars of the show, but a good show requires a strong supporting cast. Modifiers are not intended to mask the flavor of the alcohol; rather, they work with spirits and liqueurs to achieve the right flavor balance in a drink.

Sweeteners
- Honey
- Sugar (granulated, raw, superfine, etc.)

Fresh Fruits and Herbs
- Grapefruit
- Lemon
- Lime
- Mint
- Orange

Kitchen Staples
- Coffee
- Eggs
- Heavy cream
- Milk
- Nutmeg: Fresh whole nutmeg is best, as it contains lots of aromas from its natural oils.

Specialty Modifiers

- Cocktail cherries: Luxardo is highly recommended, but Fabbri Amarena, Woodford Reserve, and Jack Rudy also make comparable products. Avoid anything neon red.
- Ginger beer: Generally spicier than ginger ale, it has strong ginger flavors. Fever-Tree and Bundaberg are great options.
- Pomegranate juice: POM Wonderful is a good choice.
- Sparkling water
- Tonic water: Opt for a more artisanal brand with stronger quinine flavor, such as Fever-Tree or Q.

Homemade Syrups

These are three easy and versatile syrups I recommend making for cocktail recipes. Feel free to scale up or down, depending on how many cocktails you plan to make. Let the syrups cool before using. Homemade syrups can be kept refrigerated for two to three weeks.

SIMPLE SYRUP. Sugar doesn't dissolve easily in cold drinks, so making a syrup solves that problem. Simply dissolve 1 cup of sugar in 1 cup of hot water.

HONEY SYRUP. Thinning honey into a syrup helps it dissolve in cold drinks. To make, dissolve 1 cup of honey in 1 cup of warm water.

GRENADINE (POMEGRANATE SYRUP). Historically, grenadine is simply a pomegranate syrup, but many commercial varieties contain artificial flavors and added colors. You can easily make your own; heat 1 cup of fresh or bottled pomegranate juice and stir in 1 cup of sugar until fully dissolved.

CLASSIC BARTENDER'S TOOLS

Like any craft, bartending relies on the right tools to combine ingredients using proper techniques for optimal consistency, texture, and dilution.

The Essentials

SHAKER. The shaker is the essential mixing container for shaken cocktails. There are different styles of shakers (double shaker tins, Boston, Cobbler, etc.); just choose one you like the look and feel of. Industry professionals generally prefer weighted 18-ounce/28-ounce tins that fit together for working at volume, but for the home, anything will do.

MIXING GLASS. You can use a shaker tin, pint glass, or proper mixing glass with a heavy base for stirring drinks. Clear glasses allow you to see your drink as you mix, and a pour lip helps prevent spills.

From left: Shaker, jigger, mixing glass, bar spoon

STRAINER. Essential for separating loose ice from shaken and stirred drinks; the coiled Hawthorne-style strainer is the most versatile type.

JIGGER. This is a measuring tool for your liquid ingredients. Find a jigger with clear markings for at least ¼-, ½-, 1-, and 1½-ounce volumes to make your life easier. The OXO angled jigger works wonders and is less messy and easier to read than hourglass-shaped versions.

Clockwise from top left: Large ice cube mold, muddler, Microplane grater, strainer, small fine-mesh strainer, handheld citrus squeezer, Y-shaped vegetable peeler

BAR SPOON. A long-handled spoon that provides leverage when stirring cocktails.

Y-SHAPED VEGETABLE PEELER. This tool is used for all aromatic citrus-peel garnishes.

MICROPLANE GRATER. Used for grating whole nutmeg as the finishing touch. Whole nutmeg is vastly superior to pre-ground for aromatic value. You can also use this tool for zesting citrus or hard cheeses in your kitchen.

COCKTAIL PICKS. For skewering olives, cherries, etc. Toothpicks will do, but metal cocktail picks are more fun!

Optional (But Recommended!)

HANDHELD CITRUS SQUEEZER. Fresh citrus is critical for proper cocktails, and this handy tool makes easy work of squeezing citrus, especially when making drinks for a crowd. When using, make sure the cut side of the fruit faces down.

SMALL FINE-MESH STRAINER. Shaken drinks can contain shards of broken ice; a small fine-mesh strainer catches ice bits that escape the primary strainer. This technique is called "double straining."

LARGE CUBE ICE MOLDS. Large-format ice melts more slowly than smaller cubes, which is why cocktail bars often serve drinks with a large cube. Plus, it looks good!

MUDDLER. Used to smash fresh herbs or fruits to extract the oils and juices, and infuse with flavor and aroma. A flat-ended muddler (without spikes or ridges) works best.

GLASSWARE

Choosing the right glassware for your drinks is important, as presentation is a key part of the cocktail experience. Here are the most versatile glass types along with their common capacity ranges.

- Champagne flute (6 to 8 ounces)
- Collins glass / Tall cooler (12 to 16 ounces)
- Rocks glass / Double Old Fashioned (12 to 14 ounces)
- Small glasses (for punch). A punch bowl is also nice to have if you entertain often, but otherwise, any large bowl will do the trick.
- Small mug (for warm drinks)
- Small rocks glass / Single Old Fashioned (6 to 10 ounces)
- Coupe glass (5 to 7 ounces)

While each recipe has a recommended glass, feel free to use what you have, but keep these pointers in mind as you choose your drinkware.

- Stemmed glassware keeps a drink cold for longer, as you can pick up the drink without warming it through the heat of your hands.
- Wider glasses allow more of the drink's fragrance to hit your nose as you sip, so they are a great choice for drinks with aromatic garnishes. Narrower openings help bubbly drinks retain carbonation better.
- For the most part, cocktails should fill the glass so that it looks full and inviting, rather than half drunk. For drinks served with ice, you can add more ice at the end if it's not quite full. For drinks without additional ice, choose the smallest glass that will comfortably hold the drink.

- Straws should be used only when necessary. Funneling the drink through a tiny tube limits how the drink hits your tongue and your overall perception of taste. Additionally, straws increase the distance between your nose and the drink, which minimizes the effectiveness of aromatic garnishes.

CHAMPAGNE FLUTE

COLLINS GLASS

ROCKS GLASS

COUPE

SMALL MUG

SMALL ROCKS GLASS

SMALL GLASS (FOR PUNCH)

THE TECHNIQUES

Here are some basic techniques the home bartender can perfect for delicious results with minimal effort.

Shaking

Shaking is a fun technique that impacts a cocktail's consistency and flavor. Shaking has three objectives:

MIX. When citrus juices or cloudy ingredients (eggs, dairy) are used, shaking ensures everything is fully integrated.

AERATE. Vigorous shaking introduces tons of tiny air bubbles, which gives the cocktail a lighter mouthfeel.

CHILL AND DILUTE. A drink's temperature and flavor intensity change how flavor is perceived. Typically, you want a very cold drink with approximately 30 percent of the total volume coming from melted ice.

To shake a drink

1. Add all liquid ingredients to the shaker tin *before* adding ice. This allows you to prepare your ingredients without the ice melting.
2. Fill the tin to the top with ice (don't skimp!). This maximizes the surface area of ice to liquid for the ideal chill and dilution.
3. Seal and shake for 20 seconds. Hold firmly on to both sides of your shaker to avoid spillage. Shaking the tin in a horizontal position (back and forth) over your shoulder is more effective than shaking the tin vertically (up and down).
4. Strain the shaken drink into an empty glass or a glass filled with fresh ice. Fresh ice will melt more slowly than the used, broken-up ice and will keep your drink colder and less watered down.

Stirring

Stirring is the less dramatic method for mixing cocktails. Like shaking, stirring achieves three specific objectives:

MIX. When citrus juices and cloudy ingredients aren't used, stirring is sufficient to achieve the desired level of integration.

CREATE A SILKY TEXTURE. Stirring a drink will not introduce air bubbles. This results in a smoother, silkier mouthfeel, ideal for more richly flavored or spirit-forward drinks.

CHILL AND DILUTE. Take your time here—you're aiming not just to combine ingredients, but also to bring down the temperature and reach the ideal dilution level.

To stir a drink

1. Add all liquid ingredients to the mixing glass.
2. Fill the glass three-quarters full with ice.
3. With a gentle grip, stir in a circular motion for at least 40 seconds. The bar spoon should rest between your middle and ring fingers, and the round side of the spoon should contact the walls of the glass as you stir. During this process your hand and arm should be mostly still. The swirling motion can be accomplished by gently pushing your fingers against the handle of the spoon. It can be helpful to watch some video demonstrations to understand what the motion looks like. This will get easier as you practice.
4. Strain the stirred drink into your serving glass.

Building

Some drinks can simply be "built" in the serving glass. These types of drinks often include a notable volume of non-alcoholic ingredients (sparkling water, ginger beer, etc.) and don't require as much dilution up front. To build a drink, add all the ingredients to your serving glass, then fill to the top with ice. Stir with a bar spoon until the ice is distributed evenly in the glass.

Preparing Citrus Peels

Some cocktails call for a citrus peel as a garnish. Instead of a thin twist, I will most often use a wide swath of peel because it contains more aromatic oils. Releasing, or expressing, the oils from the peel on top of the drink plays a critical role, as the perfumed oils greet your nose and enhance the taste of the drink.

Since citrus from the grocery store can be sprayed with pesticides, try to buy organic when possible, and wash the outer skin well before using.

To cut the peel, use a Y-shaped vegetable peeler and cut a long, thick piece, approximately an inch wide and 2 to 3 inches long. Try to avoid getting too much of the bitter white pith.

To express the peel, hold it with both hands with the outer side facing toward the glass. Gently squeeze the peel in half to release a spray of fine oils on the surface of the drink, then gently rub the spent peel along the rim of the glass to deposit any remaining oils. Depending on the recipe, you can then discard the peel or drop it into the drink to further diffuse flavor.

WORKING WITH EGGS

Raw eggs* are a key ingredient for some classic cocktails. When vigorously agitated, egg whites form a semi-solid foamy top layer on a drink. Whole eggs also achieve this to some degree, but the yolk also emulsifies, resulting in a richer and creamier concoction.

To properly integrate the egg, you'll need to shake longer and more aggressively than for your usual shaken cocktails. Another popular technique for egg cocktails is a "dry shake." This process requires two rounds of shaking. In the first round, shake all the ingredients in your cocktail without ice for 20 seconds, ensuring you hold your tins tightly as it's harder to form a tight seal without ice. Following this round, add the ice to the tin and shake as normal for 20 seconds. Strain your egg cocktails the same way you would any other shaken cocktail. At first, you may not see an obvious foam layer, but give it a minute and the top layer will separate.

Final note: Modern eggs are much larger than the eggs of 100 years ago. Since it's nearly impossible to separate an egg in half, don't worry about it if you're just making one drink. However, if you're doubling the recipe, you can use a single egg for both portions.

*The USDA and CDC advise against consuming raw or undercooked eggs, so proceed at your own risk. You can also use aquafaba (the liquid from a can of chickpeas) as an egg white substitute, about one ounce per drink.

Muddling

Muddling extracts the oils or juices from fresh herbs or fruits. You'll generally muddle your ingredient with the sugar or syrup in the recipe.

When muddling delicate herbs like mint, be careful not to pulverize the leaves; otherwise, they will taste bitter. Gently press the leaves with the back of a spoon or a muddler, just enough to release the oils. This is best done in the serving glass, as shaking with ice will release unpleasant flavors.

For citrus, both the fruit and peel are important. Place the cut citrus peel-side up in a shaker or glass and gently press with your muddler to release the juices and aromatic oils. For soft fruits, like berries and stone fruits, cut into small pieces and briefly press. When shaking, the ice will extend the muddling effect.

RULES TO MIX AND IMBIBE BY

Here are a few things to keep in mind to help you make professional-caliber drinks in the comfort of your home:

FRESH IS KEY. Don't be tempted to substitute fresh citrus juice with anything that comes in a bottle. The oils and acids in citrus break down once exposed to air, so preprocessed juices will result in a completely different drink.

ICE IS AN INGREDIENT. A properly chilled drink includes about 30 percent water from melted ice, so if your ice has odd flavors from your freezer it will affect the flavor of your cocktail. The dilution from ice melt is also important to balance a cocktail, allowing flavors from high-proof spirits to open up.

MEASURE, MEASURE, MEASURE. Precise measurement can make or break a drink. You'll almost always see professional bartenders use jiggers to ensure consistency.

THE QUALITY OF YOUR ALCOHOL MATTERS. While you don't need to buy the most expensive bottles for cocktails, most of the classics are spirit-forward, which means the alcohol is a large component of the flavor. Make sure it's something you'd enjoy even on its own.

GARNISHES AREN'T JUST FOR LOOKS. Citrus peels add a layer of complexity when their oils are expressed over your glass rim; likewise, sprigs of mint greet your nose to infuse freshness into each sip. If a recipe calls for a garnish, it's often not just for decoration. That said, feel free to experiment with additional decorative garnishes.

WE DRINK FIRST WITH OUR EYES. Research shows that a drink's physical appearance can drastically impact how we perceive its taste. Mix to impress and always consider presentation! Make your garnishes both functional and beautiful, and always select the right glassware. Nothing tastes quite as good in a plastic cup.

CONSIDER JOINING A COCKTAIL COMMUNITY. Seek out communities on Instagram, YouTube, Reddit, and other platforms to share ideas and find inspiration. My inboxes are always open (see resources, page 180).

SCALING FOR A CROWD

When serving cocktails to groups, pre-batching is the way to go. After all, you don't want to spend all your time making drinks instead of socializing! Here are some best practices:

INDIVIDUAL COCKTAILS

For drinks without fresh citrus juice, simply scale up the ingredients and add about 30 percent additional water to account for the missing ice melt as you're chilling the drink. Refrigerate for a few hours up to a few days before the event, and you can serve this directly from the fridge.

For drinks that do include fresh citrus juice, it's best to add the juice shortly before serving. Scale up and premix all other ingredients, but don't add the citrus until a few hours before serving. When ready to serve, measure out individual portions of the recipe and shake with ice to properly integrate the citrus juices.

PUNCH BOWLS

A good alternative to individual cocktails is a communal punch bowl. Punches usually include citrus, so it's best to prepare them no earlier than six hours prior to serving to avoid the degradation of fresh citrus acidity (see Rules to Mix and Imbibe By, page 31). Scale up as needed, stir the ingredients, and refrigerate.

When ready to serve, add large blocks of ice to make sure the punch stays chilled without getting too watered down. Use a small pot or wide plastic container as an ice mold for large blocks of ice.

ABOUT THE COCKTAILS

Now that we've gone over how to build out your home bar and the basic techniques and rules, let's make some cocktails! The recipes in the following chapters are organized by their primary base spirit, but you can also refer to the index (page 183) to look up specific cocktails.

Selecting the Classics

The 75 recipes in this book are just the tip of the iceberg. This collection represents classic cocktails that have stood the test of time and can all be made with a limited set of bottles and fresh ingredients.

While cocktails like the Mai Tai, Bloody Mary, and Piña Colada are indeed classics, they're not included in this book because they require one or more specialty ingredients that may be less accessible or versatile for regular use across a wide array of drinks. If you find yourself truly bitten by the cocktail bug and want to expand your repertoire, check out the resources section (page 180).

Classic cocktail recipes appear in countless historical and modern publications, so what you see in this book may differ slightly from what you find in another source. For this book, my goal was to stay true to the historical intent of the recipe, adjusting as needed to adapt the drink to the modern palate.

How to Use the Recipes

Each recipe contains labels to indicate the type of glassware it's best served in and its construction method (shaken, stirred, muddled, or built). Recipes labeled "Few Ingredients" require four or fewer ingredients and will be the easiest and quickest drinks to make.

Ice is not included in the ingredient list, as it's used in almost every recipe. You'll need a generous amount of ice for proper cocktail dilution, so make sure to have lots of it on hand. Most recipes do not require adding extra water outside of ice, but those that do specifically list it.

Each recipe includes a hint, modern twist, or throwback. Hints provide insights to help you better understand and re-create the drink as you would find it at a craft cocktail bar. Modern twists include fun ideas inspired by the classic; conversely, throwbacks are suggestions to give you an idea of what the original drink may have tasted like back in the day.

The ultimate goal is to make something you enjoy. The recipe ratios shared in this book are not the only way to make these drinks, but rather provide a jumping-off point for you to experience a representative version of the cocktail. Once you've tried the recipe as written, feel free to experiment to find your perfect version of the classic.

GIN

Clockwise from top left: Gin Rickey, Martini, Gin Fizz, Martinez

BEE'S KNEES

SERVES 1 · COUPE · FEW INGREDIENTS

This simple classic was likely invented during Prohibition. Many Prohibition-era drinks were gin-based, as they were easy to concoct secretly by adding juniper flavors to watered-down grain alcohol or moonshine. Sweeteners were added to make it palatable. Thankfully, today's spirits are delicious, and when you mix a good gin with the classic combination of lemon and honey, it's easy to see how this drink has withstood the test of time.

TOOLS	INGREDIENTS
Shaker	2 ounces gin
Jigger	1 ounce honey syrup (page 20)
Strainer	
Coupe glass	¾ ounce fresh lemon juice

1. In a shaker, combine the gin, honey syrup, and lemon juice, then fill the shaker with ice. Seal and shake for 20 seconds.
2. Strain into a coupe glass.

MODERN TWIST: *One of the best ways to experiment here is to simply switch out the gin. A London Dry gin is the default for classic gin cocktails, but contemporary gins can vary dramatically in flavor profile and create vastly different cocktails.*

HINT: It's a personal preference whether you want to place a skewered cocktail cherry on the rim of the glass or inside the glass. The cherry will be coated with a layer of syrup, so placing it inside the drink will diffuse some syrup into the drink, while placing it on top lets you taste the cocktail plain first.

BIJOU

CLASSIC COCKTAILS DONE WELL

SERVES 1 · COUPE

The Bijou is a full-flavored herbaceous cocktail dating back to the late 1800s. This sweet and aromatically complex drink is perfect as a post-dinner dessert or nightcap. Older recipes call for equal parts gin, sweet vermouth, and Green Chartreuse, which result in a sweet, heavy drink. This recipe dials down the Green Chartreuse to better adapt to the modern palate. If you enjoy this drink, you may also enjoy the Martinez (page 62) or the similar whiskey-based Tipperary (page 102).

TOOLS	INGREDIENTS
Mixing glass	1 ounce gin
Jigger	1 ounce sweet vermouth
Bar spoon	¾ ounce Green Chartreuse
Strainer	2 dashes orange bitters
Coupe glass	Lemon peel, for garnish
Peeler	Cocktail cherry, for garnish
Cocktail pick	

1. In a mixing glass, combine the gin, vermouth, Green Chartreuse, and bitters, then fill the glass three-quarters full with ice. Stir for 40 seconds.
2. Strain into a coupe glass.
3. Express the oils from the lemon peel over the top of the drink, rub the peel along the rim of the glass, then drop the peel into the drink.
4. Skewer the cocktail cherry on a pick and place it inside the glass.

GIN

BRONX

SERVES 1 · COUPE

This drink was likely named for the Bronx Zoo when it opened in 1899 and is a bit like an orange Martini. It's relatively dry and spirit-forward, yet very fruity. Some modern adaptations increase the orange juice for an even fruitier drink, but the following recipe is closer to the original.

TOOLS
Shaker
Jigger
Strainer
Coupe glass
Peeler

INGREDIENTS
2 ounces gin
1 ounce sweet vermouth
1 ounce dry vermouth
¼ ounce fresh orange juice
2 dashes orange bitters
Orange peel, for garnish

1. In a shaker, combine the gin, sweet and dry vermouths, orange juice, and bitters, then fill the shaker with ice. Seal and shake for 20 seconds.
2. Strain into a coupe glass.
3. Express the oils from the orange peel over the top of the drink, rub the peel along the rim of the glass, then drop the peel into the drink.

HINT: *While this drink incorporates all dimensions of the orange—fresh juice, bitters, and peel—if you're missing any of those, don't sweat it; the drink will still be delicious.*

CLASSIC COCKTAILS DONE WELL

GIN

CLOVER CLUB

SERVES 1 · COUPE

The Clover Club, a fruity sour-style cocktail dating to the late 1800s, was enjoyed by socialites of the day. Pink used to be a color representing masculinity, but by the mid-1900s, the pink drink was regarded as a "lady's drink" and fell out of fashion. Fortunately, this drink has made a comeback in the modern cocktail revival era.

TOOLS
Shaker
Jigger
Strainer
Coupe glass

INGREDIENTS
2 ounces gin
¾ ounce fresh lemon juice
½ ounce simple syrup (page 20)
¼ ounce grenadine (page 20)
1 egg white

1. In a shaker, combine the gin, lemon juice, simple syrup, grenadine, and the egg white, then fill the shaker with ice. Seal and shake vigorously for 40 seconds to integrate the egg white thoroughly. Alternatively, you can do a dry shake first (see Working with Eggs, page 30).
2. Strain into a coupe glass.

MODERN TWIST: *Instead of grenadine, you can use muddled fresh berries or even a berry jam. For fresh berries, muddle in half a handful before adding the remaining ingredients to the shaker; for jam, add 1 teaspoon.*

FRENCH 75

SERVES 1 · CHAMPAGNE FLUTE · FEW INGREDIENTS

The French 75 is bubbly, refreshing, and sophisticated. It's essentially a Gin Fizz (page 56) with sparkling wine and is usually served in a Champagne flute. Perfect for brunch, it's easily batched to serve a crowd. To batch, use a blender to combine the gin, lemon juice, and syrup, then refrigerate. Right before serving, add the sparkling wine to the chilled mix and give it a quick stir.

TOOLS	INGREDIENTS
Shaker	2 ounces gin
Jigger	¾ ounce fresh lemon juice
Strainer	¾ ounce simple syrup (page 20)
Champagne flute	
Bar spoon	4 ounces sparkling wine
Peeler	Lemon peel, for garnish

1. In a shaker, combine the gin, lemon juice, and simple syrup, then fill the shaker with ice. Seal and shake for 20 seconds.
2. Strain into a Champagne flute.
3. Top with the sparkling wine and give it a brief stir.
4. Express the oils from the lemon peel over the top of the drink, rub the peel along the rim of the glass, then drop the peel into the drink.

MODERN TWIST: *Use a sparkling rosé wine and place some sliced strawberries inside the glass for a pink-hued, berry version!*

GIN & IT

SERVES 1 · COUPE · FEW INGREDIENTS

The classic Gin & It, sometimes known as the Sweet Martini, is made like a dry Martini but with sweet vermouth instead. The name is short for "Gin and Italian Vermouth," later shortened to just "Gin and It." True to its name, it requires only two ingredients and was popularly enjoyed without ice, which wasn't readily available in the early days. This couldn't be easier to make and tastes more complex than it might seem. A superb option for those who enjoy herbal, spirit-forward drinks like the Martini (page 63) and Martinez (page 62).

TOOLS
Mixing glass
Jigger
Bar spoon
Strainer
Coupe glass

INGREDIENTS
2 ounces gin
1 ounce sweet vermouth

1. In a mixing glass, combine the gin and vermouth, then fill the glass three-quarters full with ice. Stir for 40 seconds.
2. Strain into a coupe glass.

THROWBACK: *Some classic versions of this drink include an orange twist, orange bitters, or a slice of orange. The drink ratio has ranged anywhere from 1:4 to 4:1 in published recipes over the decades, so experiment with your proportions. You can also try it old school and skip the ice altogether.*

CLASSIC COCKTAILS DONE WELL

GIN

GIN & TONIC

SERVES 1 · COLLINS GLASS · FEW INGREDIENTS

Preparing the optimal serve of this popular drink includes using a thoughtfully selected gin paired with high-quality tonic water and decorated with beautiful aromatics (herbs, spices, fruits, edible flowers) to produce a scent bouquet for each sip. Consider choosing garnishes that match the ingredients in your chosen gin to pull out those flavor profiles. It's important for this drink to be ice-cold.

TOOLS	INGREDIENTS
Collins glass	2 ounces gin
Jigger	4 to 5 ounces tonic water
Bar spoon	Aromatic herbs, such as rosemary, lavender, sage, or basil, for garnish

1. Fill a collins glass with ice.
2. Add the gin and tonic water, then give it a quick stir.
3. Place your aromatics of choice inside the glass.

HINT: *Try serving your G&T in a large, stemmed wine glass. It's a beautiful way to showcase the clear drink and colorful aromatics. The bowl shape is also effective for directing fragrance to your nose with each sip.*

This buck style of drink (spirit, ginger, and citrus) was popularly enjoyed in the early 1900s, with the gin version being the top choice during that time. This easy drink has flexible proportions and is refreshing on a hot day.

TOOLS
Rocks glass
Jigger
Bar spoon

INGREDIENTS
2 ounces gin
½ ounce fresh lemon juice
4 ounces ginger beer
Lemon wedge, for garnish

1. Fill a rocks glass with ice.
2. Add the gin and lemon juice, then top with the ginger beer.
3. Give it a quick stir to combine and place the lemon wedge inside the glass.

HINT: *Since ginger beer constitutes a significant portion of this drink, your choice of brand will significantly impact the flavor. For something spicy and distinctively ginger, Fever-Tree ginger beer is unmatched. For something milder, try Bundaberg. Experiment with different brands to find your favorite.*

GIN DAISY

CLASSIC COCKTAILS DONE WELL

SERVES 1 · COUPE

The Gin Daisy is a refreshing afternoon sipper that was a popular drink in the late 1800s. It's similar to a Gin Fizz (page 56) but adds a bit of liqueur to make things interesting. Throughout historical recipe books, you can find daisy recipes with orange cordials, grenadine, and even more herbaceous liqueurs. The recipe below represents the oldest style, with orange liqueur.

TOOLS	INGREDIENTS
Shaker	2 ounces gin
Jigger	¾ ounce fresh lemon juice
Strainer	½ ounce simple syrup (page 20)
Coupe glass	¼ ounce orange liqueur
Bar spoon	2 ounces sparkling water

1. In a shaker, combine the gin, lemon juice, simple syrup, and orange liqueur, then fill the shaker with ice. Seal and shake for 20 seconds.
2. Strain into a coupe glass.
3. Top with the sparkling water and give it a brief stir.

   MODERN TWIST: *There are many innovative ways to adapt this drink. Try substituting the orange liqueur with grenadine (page 20) or any other specialty liqueurs you might have on hand (elderflower, raspberry, etc.). Add a sprig of mint, fresh rosemary, or a few sage leaves for extra garden freshness!*

GIN

GIN FIZZ

SERVES 1 · SMALL ROCKS GLASS · FEW INGREDIENTS

The classic Gin Fizz from the late 1800s is one of the foundational drinks in the world of cocktails and has inspired numerous historic and modern variations. This is a refreshingly balanced drink with just a hint of bubbles. *SEE PAGE 36 FOR PHOTO.*

TOOLS	INGREDIENTS
Shaker	2 ounces gin
Jigger	¾ ounce fresh lemon juice
Strainer	¼ ounce simple syrup
Small rocks glass	(page 20)
Bar spoon	1 ounce sparkling water
Peeler	Lemon peel, for garnish

1. In a shaker, combine the gin, lemon juice, and simple syrup, then fill the shaker with ice. Seal and shake for 20 seconds.
2. Strain into a small rocks glass.
3. Top with the sparkling water and give it a brief stir.
4. Express the oils from the lemon peel over the top of the drink, rub the peel along the rim of the glass, then drop the peel into the drink.

   HINT: *This recipe is the basis for other classic fizzes. By adding an egg white, this becomes a Silver Fizz. If you add an egg yolk, you'll have a Golden Fizz. A bit of mint makes this a South Side Fizz.*

CLASSIC COCKTAILS DONE WELL

GIN

GIN RICKEY

SERVES 1 · COLLINS GLASS · FEW INGREDIENTS

Although sweeteners show up frequently in cocktails, there are some classics that fully omit them. If you're looking for a low-carb option, put away your diet mixers and vodka sodas, and give this Gin Rickey a try! You'll find it refreshingly crisp and perfect for a hot day. *SEE PAGE 36 FOR PHOTO.*

CLASSIC COCKTAILS DONE WELL

TOOLS
Collins glass
Jigger
Bar spoon

INGREDIENTS
2 ounces gin
½ ounce fresh lime juice
4 ounces sparkling water
Lime wedge, for garnish

1. Fill a collins glass with ice.
2. Add the gin and lime juice, then top with the sparkling water. Give it a quick stir to combine.
3. Drop in the lime wedge to allow the peel's oils to diffuse into the drink as you sip.

   MODERN TWIST: *Sugar is a well-known flavor enhancer in cocktails, but salt is great too! Try adding a pinch of salt when stirring this cocktail to further intensify the delicate aromas of the gin and lime.*

GIN

IDEAL COCKTAIL

SERVES 1 · COUPE · FEW INGREDIENTS

This drink dates back to the early 1900s, before Prohibition, and remained well known after its repeal as well. The herbal flavors of the sweet vermouth and maraschino liqueur stand out in this drink, making it a nice pairing with a heavier meal or as a post-dinner cocktail. If you enjoy drinks like the Martinez (page 62) or Gin & It (page 49), the Ideal Cocktail should be right up your alley.

TOOLS

Shaker
Jigger
Strainer
Coupe glass

INGREDIENTS

1½ ounces gin
¾ ounce sweet vermouth
¼ ounce fresh grapefruit juice
1 bar spoonful Luxardo
   maraschino liqueur

1. In a shaker, combine the gin, vermouth, grapefruit juice, and maraschino liqueur, then fill the shaker with ice. Seal and shake for 20 seconds.
2. Strain into a coupe glass.

THROWBACK: *Some historical recipes call for dry vermouth instead of sweet, so if you prefer something on the drier side, give that swap a try.*

GIN

LAST WORD

SERVES 1 · COUPE · FEW INGREDIENTS

This pre-Prohibition cocktail became a cult favorite after being redis-covered and reintroduced in the early 2000s at Seattle's famed Zig Zag Cafe. Its renewed popularity in the twenty-first century has quickly spread to cocktail menus around the world.

TOOLS

Shaker

Jigger

Strainer

Coupe glass

INGREDIENTS

¾ ounce gin

¾ ounce fresh lime juice

¾ ounce Luxardo
maraschino liqueur

¾ ounce Green Chartreuse

1. In a shaker, combine the gin, lime juice, maraschino liqueur, and Green Chartreuse, then fill the shaker with ice. Seal and shake for 20 seconds.

2. Strain into a coupe glass.

MODERN TWIST: *This equal-parts cocktail has inspired endless modern combinations, such as the Paper Plane (bourbon, lemon juice, Aperol, Amaro Nonino), Final Ward (rye, lemon juice, Green Chartreuse, maraschino liqueur), and Naked & Famous (mezcal, lime, Aperol, Yellow Chartreuse). Experiment by substi-tuting one or two of the four ingredients—think lemon for lime, bourbon for gin, or another herbal liqueur for the maraschino liqueur or Chartreuse.*

MARTINEZ

SERVES 1 · COUPE

This drink may actually predate the famed Martini. Even with the resurgence of other popular historical cocktails, somehow this one has remained under the radar. Compared to its peers, the Martinez is more spirit-forward and complex than a Martini (page 63), but not as heavy as a Negroni (page 65) or Manhattan (page 90). It's a true classic to add to your cocktail knowledge base. SEE PAGE 36 FOR PHOTO.

TOOLS	INGREDIENTS
Mixing glass	2 ounces gin
Jigger	1½ ounces sweet vermouth
Bar spoon	¼ ounce Luxardo maraschino liqueur
Strainer	
Coupe glass	2 dashes Angostura aromatic bitters
Peeler	
	Lemon peel, for garnish

1. In a mixing glass, combine the gin, vermouth, maraschino liqueur, and bitters, then fill the glass three-quarters full with ice. Stir for 40 seconds.
2. Strain into a coupe glass.
3. Express the oils from the lemon peel over the top of the drink, rub the peel along the rim of the glass, then drop the peel into the drink.

HINT: *Sweet vermouths vary across brands. Dolin Rouge is lighter in body, Carpano Antica Formula has a heavier vanilla pull, and Punt e Mes has extra bitterness. Your choice will impact your drink's flavor profile.*

MARTINI

SERVES 1 · COUPE · FEW INGREDIENTS

The ubiquitous Martini has seen its share of variations over the years. Born in the 1880s, it has taken many forms, but today, the Martini is most recognizably a gin drink accented with dry vermouth—stirred, not shaken. SEE PAGE 36 FOR PHOTO.

TOOLS
Mixing glass
Jigger
Bar spoon
Strainer
Coupe glass
Peeler (optional)
Cocktail pick (optional)

INGREDIENTS
2 ounces gin
¼ ounce dry vermouth
Lemon peel or olives,
    for garnish

1. In a mixing glass, combine the gin and vermouth, then fill the glass three-quarters full with ice. Stir for 40 seconds.
2. Strain into a coupe glass.
3. Express the oils from the lemon peel over the top of the drink, rub the peel along the rim of the glass, then drop the peel into the drink. Alternatively, skewer 1 to 3 olives on a cocktail pick and place it carefully inside the glass.

HINT: *The ratio of gin to vermouth is a personal choice. Experiment to find your perfect balance. Well-loved ratios range anywhere from 10:1 to 1:1. With more vermouth, you'll have a softer drink with less bite, and with more gin, a more herbaceous spirit-forward drink. As for olive choice, it's all about personal preference. I love Castelvetrano, a buttery mild green olive.*

NEGRONI

SERVES 1 · ROCKS GLASS · FEW INGREDIENTS

Debate circulates over the true origin of the classic Negroni. Popular in Italy in the early twentieth century, it was enjoyed as an aperitivo: a drink meant to stimulate the appetite before a meal. On its own, Campari can be an acquired taste due to its medicinal, bitter citrus peel intensity, but it's really the defining flavor in the Negroni and its siblings—the Americano (page 159), Negroni Sbagliato (page 174), and Boulevardier (page 76).

TOOLS

Rocks glass
Mixing glass
Jigger
Bar spoon
Strainer

INGREDIENTS

1 ounce gin
1 ounce Campari
1 ounce sweet vermouth
½ slice of orange

1. Fill a rocks glass with ice or one large cube.
2. In a mixing glass, combine the gin, Campari, and vermouth, then fill the mixing glass three-quarters full with ice. Stir for 40 seconds.
3. Strain into the ice-filled rocks glass and place the slice of orange inside the glass.

MODERN TWIST: *Create a Strawberry Negroni by using strawberry-infused Campari. Fill a jar with sliced strawberries, then top off with Campari. After a few days at room temperature, strain the mixture to remove all solids. If well strained, this will keep in the refrigerator for two to three months.*

PINK LADY

CLASSIC COCKTAILS DONE WELL

SERVES 1 · COUPE

The Pink Lady is a reincarnation of the classic Clover Club (page 45), with even more fruitiness, thanks to the addition of apple brandy. Like the Clover Club, this drink eventually became known as a "lady's drink" and lost popularity before its revival in the modern cocktail era. With a beautiful color, fruity-yet-spirited balance, and a cloud of foam, the Pink Lady is sure to impress all genders alike.

TOOLS	INGREDIENTS
Shaker	1½ ounces gin
Jigger	½ ounce apple brandy
Strainer	½ ounce fresh lemon juice
Coupe glass	¼ ounce grenadine (page 20)
	¼ ounce simple syrup (page 20)
	1 egg white

1. In a shaker, combine the gin, apple brandy, lemon juice, grenadine, simple syrup, and the egg white, then fill the shaker with ice. Seal and shake vigorously for 40 seconds to integrate the egg white thoroughly. Alternatively, you can do a dry shake first (see Working with Eggs, page 30).

2. Strain into a coupe glass.

HINT: *When working with egg whites, separate the white from the yolk over a bowl to avoid accidentally dropping yolk into your shaker full of ingredients.*

GIN

TOM COLLINS

SHAKEN

SERVES 1 · COLLINS · FEW INGREDIENTS

Before this drink was called the Tom Collins, it was a John Collins. Who are Tom and John? The original drink was popularized by a headwaiter named John Collins from a famous London hotel and utilized genever, a heavier spirit with a similar botanical profile to gin. The drink eventually morphed into the Tom Collins; "Tom" referring to the adoption of Old Tom gin instead of genever. Old Tom gin was sweeter than the now-popular London Dry style.

CLASSIC COCKTAILS DONE WELL

TOOLS

Shaker
Jigger
Collins glass
Strainer
Bar spoon

INGREDIENTS

2 ounces gin
¾ ounce fresh lemon juice
½ ounce simple syrup
(page 20)
3 ounces sparkling water
Lemon slice, for garnish

1. In a shaker, combine the gin, lemon juice, and simple syrup, then fill the shaker with ice. Seal and shake for 20 seconds.
2. Fill a collins glass with fresh ice, then strain the drink into the glass.
3. Top with the sparkling water and give it a brief stir.
4. Place the lemon slice inside the glass.

MODERN TWIST: *Vegetables can make a wonderful addition to this cocktail! Try muddling a few slices of cucumber, bell pepper (any color), or snap peas in your shaker before shaking.*

GIN

TUXEDO

SERVES 1 · COUPE

Most historically documented recipes for the Tuxedo include some combination of maraschino liqueur, absinthe, and orange bitters; a few utilize dry sherry. This early 1900s drink is an elevated, more herbaceous Martini (page 63).

TOOLS

Coupe glass
Mixing glass
Jigger
Bar spoon
Strainer
Peeler

INGREDIENTS

Absinthe, for rinse
2 ounces gin
1 ounce dry vermouth
1 bar spoonful Luxardo maraschino liqueur
1 dash orange bitters
Lemon peel, for garnish

1. Add a few drops of absinthe to the coupe glass, swirl to coat the glass, then empty the excess.
2. In a mixing glass, combine the gin, vermouth, maraschino liqueur, and bitters, then fill the glass three-quarters full with ice. Stir for 40 seconds.
3. Strain into the coupe glass.
4. Express the oils from the lemon peel over the top of the drink, rub the peel along the rim of the glass, then drop the peel into the drink.

HINT: *Since absinthe can be overpowering, using it to rinse the glass instead of adding it directly to the drink can help prevent accidentally using too much. If you use it often, consider getting a small atomizer bottle to house your absinthe. You can use a spray to finish off a drink for an extra aromatic boost!*

WHITE LADY

SERVES 1 · COUPE · FEW INGREDIENTS

The White Lady is a 1920s citrusy gin sour. It's like the Sidecar (page 129), but the brandy is replaced with gin and there is no sugar rim (although you're free to add one). Depending on the sweetness of your orange liqueur, you may want to adjust the amount of simple syrup.

TOOLS	INGREDIENTS
Shaker	2 ounces gin
Jigger	½ ounce fresh lemon juice
Strainer	½ ounce orange liqueur
Coupe glass	¼ ounce simple syrup (page 20)

1. In a shaker, combine the gin, lemon juice, orange liqueur, and simple syrup, then fill the shaker with ice. Seal and shake for 20 seconds.
2. Strain into a coupe glass.

MODERN TWIST: *This drink is often made with the addition of an egg white for a richer mouthfeel. Just add the egg white to your shaker with the other ingredients, then shake vigorously for about 40 seconds before straining. Alternatively, you can do a dry shake first (see Working with Eggs, page 30).*

WHISKEY

Clockwise from top left: Ward Eight, Gold Rush, De La Louisiane, Whiskey Sling

BOULEVARDIER

SERVES 1 · ROCKS GLASS · FEW INGREDIENTS

This deeply flavored, bitter-yet-warming spirit-forward drink first appeared in the 1927 publication of *Barflies and Cocktails*, using equal parts Campari, Italian sweet vermouth, and bourbon. Today's Boulevardiers are usually made with more whiskey, often rye, to provide a spicier counterpart to the Campari and sweet vermouth.

TOOLS
Rocks glass
Mixing glass
Jigger
Bar spoon
Strainer
Peeler

INGREDIENTS
1½ ounces bourbon or rye whiskey
¾ ounce Campari
¾ ounce sweet vermouth
Orange peel, for garnish

1. Fill a rocks glass with ice or one large cube.
2. In a mixing glass, combine the whiskey, Campari, and vermouth, then fill the glass three-quarters full with ice. Stir for 40 seconds.
3. Strain into the ice-filled rocks glass.
4. Express the oils from the orange peel over the top of the drink, rub the peel along the rim of the glass, then drop the peel into the drink.

HINT: *You'll sometimes see sweet (red) vermouth referred to as "Italian vermouth" and dry vermouth referred to as "French vermouth." Today, sweet and dry styles are both made by Italian and French producers. However, when re-creating classic recipes, it's still a good bet to use historic brands (see page 18).*

BROWN DERBY

SERVES 1 · COUPE · FEW INGREDIENTS

The Brown Derby is sweet, slightly citrus, and surprisingly spirit-forward—perfect when you're looking for a cocktail that's not too light yet not too spirituous. This hits the mark with the fresh aroma from the grapefruit and a strong backbone of whiskey, foregoing the tart zing you usually get from lemons and limes.

TOOLS

Shaker

Jigger

Strainer

Coupe glass

INGREDIENTS

2 ounces bourbon whiskey

1 ounce fresh grapefruit juice

¾ ounce honey syrup
(page 20)

1. In a shaker, combine the whiskey, grapefruit juice, and honey syrup, then fill the shaker with ice. Seal and shake for 20 seconds.

2. Strain into a coupe glass.

HINT: *Consider adding a strip of fresh grapefruit peel for extra brightness.*

DE LA LOUISIANE

SERVES 1 · COUPE

This early 1900s drink was the house special at the Restaurant de la Louisiane and originally called for equal parts whiskey, sweet vermouth, and Bénédictine. This revised recipe dials down the sweetness a tad but stays true to the original character of the drink—rich and full of dark fruit, with a cloud of mysterious herbal complexity. Think of it as a jazzed-up Manhattan (page 90). *SEE PAGE 74 FOR PHOTO.*

TOOLS	INGREDIENTS
Mixing glass	2 ounces rye whiskey
Jigger	¾ ounce sweet vermouth
Bar spoon	¾ ounce Bénédictine
Strainer	3 dashes Peychaud's bitters
Coupe glass	1 bar spoonful absinthe
Cocktail pick	Cocktail cherries, for garnish

1. In a mixing glass, combine the whiskey, vermouth, Bénédictine, bitters, and absinthe, then fill the glass three-quarters full with ice. Stir for 40 seconds.
2. Strain into a coupe glass.
3. Skewer a few cocktail cherries on a pick and place on the rim of the glass.

HINT: *If you use cocktail picks regularly for cherries or olives, consider getting a set of reusable metal picks. They're relatively inexpensive and come in all sorts of colors and designs. I particularly enjoy the sword-shaped picks.*

GOLD RUSH

SERVES 1 · ROCKS GLASS · FEW INGREDIENTS

The Gold Rush's golden hue and honey, citrus flavors make it a favorite for many. Although this drink sounds like it may have originated during the California Gold Rush era, it was actually created during the cocktail revival in the early 2000s. It's a simple twist on the Whiskey Sour (page 107), credited to T. J. Siegel at the celebrated Milk & Honey bar in New York City. The Gold Rush exemplifies perfection through simplicity. *SEE PAGE 74 FOR PHOTO.*

CLASSIC COCKTAILS DONE WELL

TOOLS
Rocks glass
Shaker
Jigger
Strainer

INGREDIENTS
2 ounces bourbon whiskey
1 ounce honey syrup
   (page 20)
¾ ounce fresh lemon juice

1. Fill a rocks glass with ice or one large cube.
2. In a shaker, combine the whiskey, honey syrup, and lemon juice, then fill the shaker with ice. Seal and shake for 20 seconds.
3. Strain into the ice-filled rocks glass.

MODERN TWIST: *This drink also works well with a Scotch whisky in place of bourbon.*

WHISKEY

HOT WHISKEY PUNCH

CLASSIC COCKTAILS DONE WELL

SERVES 8 · MUGS · FEW INGREDIENTS

Before individual cocktails became more popular, communal punch bowls prevailed, and knowing how to make a good punch was considered an important home entertaining skill. The secret to amazing punches is *oleo saccharum* (or "oil sugar"), a critical ingredient in historical punches. It will revolutionize your punch game!

TOOLS	INGREDIENTS
Peeler	4 medium lemons
Bowl or jar	4 ounces sugar
Muddler	16 ounces whiskey
Bar spoon	16 ounces hot water
Heat-resistant punch bowl	
Measuring cups	
Heat-resistant mugs or glasses	

1. At least 1 day before serving, prepare the lemon oleo saccharum. Use a peeler to skin your citrus, avoiding the white pith. Place the peels inside a bowl or jar and cover them with the sugar.
2. Muddle well to start the oil extraction, then cover and let it sit for up to 1 day. When you notice that the peels have shrunk in size and are covered with a thick glaze, your oleo saccharum is ready.
3. Squeeze the juice from the four peeled lemons into the liquified oleo saccharum and stir well until the sugar is dissolved.
4. Strain the peels from the oleo saccharum and lemon juice mixture, and pour the liquid into a punch bowl.
5. Add the whiskey and hot water to the bowl and stir.
6. Serve in small heat-resistant glasses or mugs.

WHISKEY

MODERN TWIST: Feel free to swap in a different spirit, add extra spices (cinnamon, cloves, nutmeg, star anise, etc.), or use hot tea in place of hot water.

HINT: I recommend storing your large ice cubes in a resealable freezer bag rather than in the ice cube mold. Uncovered ice tends to pick up unpleasant flavors from the freezer, which is not good for your drink.

IMPROVED WHISKEY COCKTAIL

SERVES 1 · ROCKS GLASS

This late 1800s drink falls between a classic Old Fashioned (page 94) and a Sazerac (page 98)—strong and whiskey-forward with pizazz. Back in the day, the Old Fashioned was just called a Whiskey Cocktail, and the "improvement" refers to the addition of absinthe and maraschino liqueur for extra depth of flavor.

TOOLS

Rocks glass

Mixing glass

Jigger

Bar spoon

Strainer

Peeler

INGREDIENTS

Absinthe, for rinse

2 ounces rye whiskey

¼ ounce simple syrup (page 20)

1 bar spoonful Luxardo maraschino liqueur

2 dashes Angostura aromatic bitters

Lemon peel, for garnish

1. Add a few drops of absinthe to a rocks glass, swirl to coat the glass, then empty the excess.
2. Fill the rocks glass with ice or one large cube.
3. In a mixing glass, combine the whiskey, simple syrup, maraschino liqueur, and bitters, then fill the glass three-quarters full with ice. Stir for 40 seconds.
4. Strain into the ice-filled rocks glass.
5. Express the oils from the lemon peel over the top of the drink, rub the peel along the rim of the glass, then drop the peel into the drink.

IRISH COFFEE

CLASSIC COCKTAILS DONE WELL

SERVES 1 · SMALL MUG

In 1952, the Irish Coffee was introduced to the United States at The Buena Vista cafe in San Francisco. You can still visit this bar and watch the bartender whip up a dozen Irish Coffees at a time. Many modern versions use Irish cream liqueurs, canned whipped cream, and other ingredients that make the drink sweeter than necessary. The original is simple and boozy and won't give you a sugar high. Freshly grated nutmeg gives it an elegant finish.

TOOLS

Jar with lid
Small mug
Jigger
Bar spoon
Microplane grater

INGREDIENTS

2 ounces heavy cream
4 ounces hot strong coffee
½ ounce simple syrup (page 20)
1½ ounces Irish whiskey
Whole nutmeg, for grating

1. In a tightly sealed jar, shake the heavy cream until visibly thick but still pourable.
2. In a mug, combine the hot coffee and simple syrup.
3. Add the whiskey and give it a gentle stir.
4. Carefully float the thickened cream on top by gently pouring it over the back of a bar spoon into the mug. Add at least ¼ to ½ inch of the cream, depending on your glass diameter.
5. Grate some nutmeg over the cream.

HINT: *If making a large batch, you can use a blender to thicken the cream. Try adding a pinch of salt to the cream for an interesting flavor contrast.*

WHISKEY

JUNIOR

SERVES 1 · COUPE · FEW INGREDIENTS

This drink was first published in a 1937 magazine and hovers in the Whiskey Sour (page 107) realm with an extra lift of botanical richness. More spirit-forward than sweet, the drink also boasts a beautiful golden pink color. This is a great drink to kick off an evening of cocktails, as it's familiar and approachable, but the herbal complexity from the Bénédictine will prepare your palate for an evening of adventure.

TOOLS
Shaker
Jigger
Strainer
Coupe glass

INGREDIENTS
2 ounces rye whiskey
½ ounce Bénédictine
½ ounce fresh lime juice
1 dash Angostura aromatic bitters

1. In a shaker, combine the whiskey, Bénédictine, lime juice, and bitters, then fill the shaker with ice. Seal and shake for 20 seconds.

2. Strain into a coupe glass.

HINT: *Measuring your ingredients is incredibly important, but here is a good rule of thumb for estimating how much citrus you'll need: One average-size lime will provide ½ to ¾ ounce of juice, and an average lemon will contain about 1 ounce of juice.*

MANHATTAN

SERVES 1 · COUPE · FEW INGREDIENTS

The Manhattan is one of the most famous whiskey cocktails and has been found in recipe books since the late 1800s. This spirit-forward drink really showcases the whiskey. Along with the Old Fashioned (page 94) and Whiskey Sour (page 107), this influential whiskey classic has inspired countless modern creations.

TOOLS

Mixing glass

Jigger

Bar spoon

Strainer

Coupe glass

Cocktail pick

INGREDIENTS

2 ounces rye whiskey

¾ ounce sweet vermouth

2 dashes Angostura
   aromatic bitters

Cocktail cherries, for garnish

1. In a mixing glass, combine the whiskey, vermouth, and bitters, then fill the glass three-quarters full with ice. Stir for 40 seconds.
2. Strain into a coupe glass.
3. Skewer a few cocktail cherries on a pick and place on the rim of the glass.

THROWBACK: *If you substitute Scotch for the rye whiskey, you now have a Rob Roy, another historical drink from around the same time. Blended and single malt Scotches will both work for this Manhattan variant. Single malts result in a richer, more full-bodied drink; typical blended Scotches produce a lighter drink.*

CLASSIC COCKTAILS DONE WELL

WHISKEY

MINT JULEP

SERVES 1 · ROCKS · FEW INGREDIENTS

The julep is a classic cocktail style that's been made using everything from brandy to gin. Today, the most common style of Mint Julep is made with bourbon whiskey. It's a refreshing drink—not too sweet and full of flavor.

TOOLS
Rocks glass
Jigger
Bar spoon
Muddler (optional)

INGREDIENTS
8 to 10 fresh mint leaves, plus more for garnish
¼ ounce simple syrup (page 20)
2 ounces bourbon whiskey

1. In a rocks glass, combine the mint and simple syrup.
2. Use a bar spoon or muddler to gently bruise the mint leaves, without pulverizing them.
3. Add the bourbon and give it a stir.
4. Fill the glass with crushed ice, then stir until the ice is settled and integrated with the liquids.
5. Add a fresh bouquet of mint on top for garnish.

HINT: *When garnishing with fresh herbs, smack them on your palm to release more of their aroma.*

OLD FASHIONED

CLASSIC COCKTAILS DONE WELL

WHISKEY

SERVES 1 · ROCKS GLASS · FEW INGREDIENTS

The Old Fashioned, one of the oldest known mixed drinks, dates back to the 1800s. Enhanced by only a bit of sugar and spice (cocktail bitters), the whiskey takes center stage. American whiskey is most often used, so feel free to experiment with either bourbon or rye. For more variety, try a Scotch or Japanese whisky, or even an Irish whiskey. Irish and Japanese styles tend to be lighter and fruitier, whereas Scotch whiskies are generally richer, maltier, and less woody than their American counterparts.

TOOLS

Rocks glass
Mixing glass
Bar spoon
Strainer
Peeler

INGREDIENTS

2 ounces bourbon whiskey
¼ ounce simple syrup (page 20)
2 dashes Angostura aromatic bitters
Orange peel, for garnish

1. Fill a rocks glass with ice or one large cube.
2. In a mixing glass, combine the whiskey, simple syrup, and bitters, then fill the mixing glass three-quarters full with ice. Stir for 40 seconds.
3. Strain into the ice-filled rocks glass.
4. Express the oils from the orange peel over the top of the drink, rub the peel along the rim of the glass, then drop the peel into the drink.

MODERN TWIST: *Replace the simple syrup with maple syrup, brown sugar syrup, or honey syrup (page 20).*

OLD PAL

CLASSIC COCKTAILS DONE WELL

SERVES 1 · COUPE · FEW INGREDIENTS

The Old Pal, another classic cocktail from the early 1900s, is a spirit-forward whiskey cocktail perfect for those who enjoy the complexity of a Manhattan (page 90) or Boulevardier (page 76), but prefer something a bit less sweet. Dry vermouth makes this drink dry and slightly savory. The drink has a hint of bitterness with a pleasant lingering flavor.

TOOLS

Mixing glass
Jigger
Bar spoon
Strainer
Coupe glass

INGREDIENTS

1½ ounces rye whiskey
¾ ounce dry vermouth
¾ ounce Campari

1. In a mixing glass, combine the whiskey, vermouth, and Campari, then fill the glass three-quarters full with ice. Stir for 40 seconds.
2. Strain into a coupe glass.

HINT: *Depending on your preference of sweetness and bitterness, you can adjust the amounts of dry vermouth and Campari to suit your palate.*

WHISKEY

SAZERAC

CLASSIC COCKTAILS DONE WELL

SERVES 1 · SMALL ROCKS GLASS

The Sazerac is one of the most famous New Orleans drinks. A Sazerac is bolder and more herbaceous than the Old Fashioned (page 94), with a strong anise kick from the absinthe and Peychaud's bitters. It's said that this drink was the Sazerac House's version of the Improved Whiskey Cocktail (page 85), but it became so popular that it gained its own identity. The Sazerac was originally made with grape brandy, but when the phylloxera epidemic destroyed most European grapevines in the late 1800s, brandy fell into short supply, opening the doors for rye to become the preferred spirit in this timeless drink.

TOOLS	INGREDIENTS
Small rocks glass	Absinthe, for rinse
Mixing glass	2 ounces rye whiskey
Jigger	¼ ounce simple syrup (page 20)
Bar spoon	
Strainer	3 dashes Peychaud's bitters
Peeler	2 dashes Angostura aromatic bitters
	Lemon peel

WHISKEY

1. Add a few drops of absinthe to a small rocks glass, swirl to coat the glass, then empty the excess.
2. In a mixing glass, combine the whiskey, simple syrup, and both bitters, then fill the glass three-quarters full with ice. Stir for 40 seconds.
3. Strain into the prepared small rocks glass.
4. Express the oils from the lemon peel over the top of the drink, rub the peel along the rim of the glass, then discard the peel.

HINT: The Sazerac explicitly calls to discard the peel rather than drop it into the drink. This practice is a defining feature of a properly made Sazerac, allowing you to enjoy the drink without distraction from a floating peel.

SEELBACH

SERVES 1 · CHAMPAGNE FLUTE

This drink was designed for the Seelbach Hotel in Louisville, Kentucky. It was believed that this was a lost-and-found recipe from the early 1900s from the hotel, but that was later discovered to be a fabricated story. Nevertheless, this bitters-heavy drink is a delightful option when you're looking for something bubbly and festive yet a bit more spice-rich and complex.

TOOLS	INGREDIENTS
Shaker	1 ounce bourbon whiskey
Jigger	½ ounce orange liqueur
Strainer	7 dashes Angostura aromatic bitters
Champagne flute	
Bar spoon	7 dashes Peychaud's bitters
Peeler	5 ounces sparkling wine
	Orange peel, for garnish

1. In a shaker, combine the bourbon, orange liqueur, and both bitters, then fill the shaker with ice. Seal and shake for 20 seconds.
2. Strain into a Champagne flute.
3. Top with the sparkling wine and give it a brief stir.
4. Express the oils from the orange peel over the top of the drink, rub the peel along the rim of the glass, then drop the peel into the drink.

HINT: *How much is a dash? This vague term is difficult to quantify. Consider a dash to be a firm downward jolt of the bitters bottle; if measured, somewhere around ⅛ teaspoon.*

TIPPERARY

SERVES 1 · COUPE · FEW INGREDIENTS

Tipperary is a county in Ireland and the namesake for this classic Irish whiskey drink. Lighter than many whiskey cocktails, this drink is similar to a Manhattan (page 90), with an additional herbal kick from the Chartreuse.

TOOLS

Mixing glass
Jigger
Bar spoon
Strainer
Coupe glass
Peeler

INGREDIENTS

2 ounces Irish whiskey
1 ounce sweet vermouth
¼ ounce Green Chartreuse
Orange peel, for garnish

1. In a mixing glass, combine the whiskey, vermouth, and Green Chartreuse, then fill the glass three-quarters full with ice. Stir for 40 seconds.
2. Strain into a coupe glass.
3. Express the oils from the orange peel over the top of the drink, rub the peel along the rim of the glass, then drop the peel into the drink.

MODERN TWIST: *Incorporating a dash of orange bitters can help further bind the flavors in this drink.*

CLASSIC COCKTAILS DONE WELL

WHISKEY

WARD EIGHT

SHAKEN

CLASSIC COCKTAILS DONE WELL

SERVES 1 · COUPE

The Ward Eight is a classic whiskey cocktail that's fruity and full of depth. This version of the Whiskey Sour (page 107) adds orange and pomegranate to the standard mix of lemon, sugar, and whiskey. The name refers to Boston's 8th ward, and the drink was supposedly created in 1898 in celebration of a political win due to the decisive vote of this ward. *SEE PAGE 74 FOR PHOTO.*

TOOLS
Shaker
Jigger
Strainer
Coupe glass
Cocktail pick

INGREDIENTS
2 ounces rye whiskey
¾ ounce fresh lemon juice
¾ ounce fresh orange juice
¼ ounce grenadine (page 20)
Cocktail cherry, for garnish

1. In a shaker, combine the whiskey, lemon juice, orange juice, and grenadine, then fill the shaker with ice. Seal and shake for 20 seconds.
2. Strain into a coupe glass.
3. Skewer a cherry on a cocktail pick and place it inside the glass.

HINT: *Using a handheld citrus press makes it easier to squeeze your citrus, plus it prevents the seeds from entering your shaker. When squeezing citrus by hand, place a fork under the fruit to catch the seeds.*

WHISKEY

104

WHISKEY SLING

SERVES 1 · ROCKS GLASS · FEW INGREDIENTS

The Sling is the predecessor to the "Cocktail" (also known as the Old Fashioned) and was a popular early 1800s American drink, consumed throughout the day, from morning to evening. The Cocktail eventually replaced the Sling as the libation of choice for imbibers, and the Sling fell into obscurity. The Cocktail is sometimes referred to as a "Bittered Sling," as it's essentially a Sling with bitters. *SEE PAGE 74 FOR PHOTO.*

TOOLS

Rocks glass
Mixing glass
Jigger
Bar spoon
Strainer
Microplane grater

INGREDIENTS

2 ounces whiskey
  (bourbon or rye)
¼ ounce simple syrup
  (page 20)
Whole nutmeg, for grating

1. Fill a rocks glass with ice or one large cube.
2. In a mixing glass, combine the whiskey and simple syrup, then fill the mixing glass three-quarters full with ice. Stir for 40 seconds.
3. Strain into the ice-filled rocks glass.
4. Grate some nutmeg over the top.

THROWBACK: *Ice did not become economically available until later in the nineteenth century, so the earliest imbibers of the Sling enjoyed it sans ice. For an ultimate classic experience, substitute the ice with 1 ounce of water.*

WHISKEY SOUR

SERVES 1 · ROCKS GLASS

A sour is a basic cocktail template consisting of a spirit accompanied by tart and sweet components. Throughout history, this drink has been adapted with egg whites, liqueurs, muddled fruits, wine, and more. This recipe presents the Whiskey Sour in its most classic form, which is fantastic as is, but also serves as a blank canvas for experimentation.

TOOLS

Rocks glass
Shaker
Jigger
Strainer
Peeler

INGREDIENTS

2 ounces whiskey
   (bourbon or rye)
¾ ounce fresh lemon juice
¾ ounce simple syrup
   (page 20)
2 dashes Angostura
   aromatic bitters
Lemon peel, for garnish

1. Fill a rocks glass with ice or one large cube.
2. In a shaker, combine the whiskey, lemon juice, simple syrup, and bitters, then fill the shaker with ice. Seal and shake for 20 seconds.
3. Strain into the ice-filled rocks glass.
4. Express the oils from the lemon peel over the top of the drink, rub the peel along the rim of the glass, then drop the peel into the drink.

MODERN TWIST: *Try adding a sprig of rosemary, thyme, or another aromatic herb to top off the drink.*

BRANDY

Clockwise from top left: Brandy Punch, Sidecar, Jack Rose

APPLE TODDY

CLASSIC COCKTAILS DONE WELL

SERVES 1 · SMALL MUG

The toddy has been enjoyed both hot and cold and constructed using different base spirits. Apple brandy was popular in eighteenth- and nineteenth-century America, making it a prime choice for a toddy. Because Angostura aromatic bitters are full of the aroma of rich baking spices (clove, nutmeg, allspice, etc.), it's a perfect addition for toddies to ramp up the flavor. This warm delight is perfect for a cold day or anytime you want to feel cozy.

TOOLS	INGREDIENTS
Small mug	2 ounces apple brandy
Jigger	½ ounce simple syrup (page 20)
Bar spoon	1 dash Angostura aromatic bitters (optional)
Microplane grater	3 ounces boiling water
	Whole nutmeg, for grating

1. In a small mug, combine the brandy, simple syrup, and bitters (if using).
2. Add the boiling water and stir to combine.
3. Grate some nutmeg over the top.

MODERN TWIST: *Try substituting honey syrup (page 20) or maple syrup in place of the simple syrup. Adding a cinnamon stick, a few slices of apple, or a slice of lemon also enhances the aroma of the drink as you sip.*

BRANDY

HINT: Wet the whole outer top inch of the glass to coat with sugar instead of just the thin top edge of the glass. This helps minimize sugar falling into the glass and provides more surface area of sugar to enjoy.

BRANDY CRUSTA

SERVES 1 · CHAMPAGNE FLUTE

Born in the mid-1800s in New Orleans, this sophisticated cocktail can be made using any base spirit, though the brandy version has endured. There are two defining characteristics of a crusta: the sugar rim and the thick band of citrus lining the inner rim of the glass. Presentation is a large part of what makes the Brandy Crusta the Brandy Crusta.

TOOLS

Small bowl

Champagne flute

Peeler

Shaker

Jigger

Strainer

INGREDIENTS

Sugar, to rim the glass

½ ounce fresh lemon juice, plus more for the rim

1 long, wide lemon peel, cut from the full circumference of the lemon

2 ounces Cognac

½ ounce orange liqueur

¼ ounce Luxardo maraschino liqueur

2 dashes Angostura aromatic bitters

1. Pour some sugar into a small bowl. Wet the edge of a Champagne flute with water or lemon juice. Dip the glass rim into the sugar bowl.

2. Carefully wrap the lemon peel around the inner walls of the glass, peel-side facing out.

3. In a shaker, combine the lemon juice, Cognac, orange liqueur, maraschino liqueur, and bitters, then fill the shaker with ice. Seal and shake for 20 seconds.

4. Strain into the prepared Champagne flute.

BRANDY FIZZ

SERVES 1 · SMALL ROCKS GLASS · FEW INGREDIENTS

Made in the same way as a Gin Fizz (page 56), the Brandy Fizz is a mild, sweet, and tart drink with a hint of sparkle, perfect for all times of the day. Historically, the fizz was meant to be consumed rather quickly, so it's not served with ice, but modern serves don't always follow this rule.

TOOLS

Shaker
Jigger
Strainer
Small rocks glass
Bar spoon

INGREDIENTS

2 ounces Cognac
¾ ounce fresh lemon juice
¾ ounce simple syrup (page 20)
1 ounce sparkling water

1. In a shaker, combine the Cognac, lemon juice, and simple syrup, then fill the shaker with ice. Seal and shake for 20 seconds.
2. Strain into a small rocks glass.
3. Top with the sparkling water and give it a brief stir.

MODERN TWIST: *Cognac is a softer spirit that plays very nicely with fruits such as strawberry or pear. To incorporate these flavors, you can muddle in a few pieces of fresh fruit before shaking. Or you can infuse the Cognac by filling a jar with cut pieces of fruit and topping it off with Cognac. After a few days, strain out the fruit. If all the solids are strained out, you don't need to worry about the infusion going bad, although the flavor may fade after some weeks.*

BRANDY OLD FASHIONED

SERVES 1 · ROCKS GLASS

While brandy's current popularity is relatively limited in most of the United States, it's extremely popular in the state of Wisconsin, which has helped put the famed Brandy Old Fashioned on the cocktail map. Some cocktail enthusiasts will say not to muddle orange and cherries into an Old Fashioned; however, the Brandy Old Fashioned requires exactly this. This drink was originally made using California-produced brandy instead of Cognac, so feel free to use either. Two great California-based options are Korbel and Germain-Robin.

TOOLS
Rocks glass
Jigger
Muddler
Bar spoon

INGREDIENTS
¼ ounce simple syrup (page 20)

2 dashes Angostura aromatic bitters

½ slice of orange

1 cocktail cherry

2 ounces Cognac or other grape brandy

1. In the rocks glass, combine the simple syrup, bitters, orange, and cherry. Muddle gently until the fruits are mostly mashed.
2. Add the Cognac and gently stir to combine.
3. Fill the glass with crushed ice.

HINT: *When muddling the orange (or any citrus with a peel), try to avoid harsh contact with the white pith, which will add unpleasant bitterness to your drink.*

BRANDY PUNCH

CLASSIC COCKTAILS DONE WELL

BRANDY

SERVES 8 · SMALL GLASSES

This cold version of the Hot Whiskey Punch (page 82) is made using brandy instead of whiskey. Brandy is milder than whiskey, with more fruity and caramel aromas compared to whiskey's oaky, spicy flavors. If you have time, chill the punch in the refrigerator for two to three hours to allow the flavors to come together. *SEE PAGE 108 FOR PHOTO.*

TOOLS	INGREDIENTS
Peeler	4 medium lemons
Bowl or jar	4 ounces sugar
Muddler	16 ounces Cognac
Bar spoon	16 ounces water
Punch bowl	Whole nutmeg, for grating
Measuring cup	
Microplane grater	
Small glasses	

1. At least 1 day before serving, prepare your lemon oleo saccharum (see page 82). Use a peeler to skin your citrus, avoiding the white pith. Place the peels inside a bowl or jar and cover them with the sugar.

2. Muddle well to start the oil extraction, then cover and let it sit for up to 1 day. When you notice that the peels have shrunk in size and are covered with a thick glaze, your oleo saccharum is ready.

3. Squeeze the juice from the four peeled lemons into the liquified oleo saccharum and stir well until the sugar is completely dissolved.

4. Strain the peels from the oleo saccharum and lemon juice mixture, and pour the liquid into a punch bowl.
5. Add the Cognac and water to the bowl and stir to combine.
6. Grate some nutmeg over the top and stir gently to combine.
7. Fill your punch bowl with large ice cubes. Adjust for taste as needed. The drink will dilute over time, so consider starting a bit on the stronger side.
8. Serve in small glasses with ice.

HINT: *You can use any kind of citrus for your oleo saccharum. Typically, I use 1 ounce of sugar per fruit for smaller fruits like lemons and limes and 2 ounces of sugar per fruit for larger fruits like grapefruits.*

CHAMPS ÉLYSÉES

SERVES 1 · COUPE

This drink is named after the famous avenue in Paris, aptly, for its inclusion of French spirits—Cognac and the historic Green Chartreuse. This boozy number first showed up in a 1925 recipe book called *Drinks Long & Short* and is an interesting adaptation of the Sidecar (page 129) with the herbal flavors from Green Chartreuse.

TOOLS
Shaker
Jigger
Strainer
Coupe glass

INGREDIENTS
2 ounces Cognac
¾ ounce fresh lemon juice
½ ounce Green Chartreuse
¼ ounce simple syrup (page 20)
1 dash Angostura aromatic bitters

1. In a shaker, combine the Cognac, lemon juice, Green Chartreuse, simple syrup, and bitters, then fill the shaker with ice. Seal and shake for 20 seconds.

2. Strain into a coupe glass.

HINT: *Some adaptations of this recipe use Yellow Chartreuse instead of Green Chartreuse since the original recipe did not specify. Flavorwise, Yellow Chartreuse is like the green version, but milder in intensity with stronger honey notes. If that sounds up your alley, consider picking up a bottle to experiment with in any recipe that includes Green Chartreuse.*

CLASSIC COCKTAILS DONE WELL

BRANDY

121

EGG FLIP

SERVES 1 · COUPE

The use of eggs in cocktails is common these days, but usually only the egg whites are used. Flips use an entire egg and are a historic classic with numerous published recipes since the 1800s. The yolk acts as an emulsifier to give the drink creaminess without dairy. Flips were sometimes served hot and sometimes cold. Hot egg flips run the risk of turning into scrambled eggs, so most flips today are served iced.

TOOLS	INGREDIENTS
Shaker	1 whole egg
Bar spoon	2 ounces Cognac
Jigger	¼ ounce simple syrup (page 20)
Strainer	
Coupe glass	¼ ounce orange liqueur
Microplane grater	Whole nutmeg, for grating

1. Crack the egg into a shaker, then break up the yolk using the bar spoon.
2. Add the Cognac, simple syrup, and orange liqueur, then fill the shaker with ice. Seal and shake very well for at least 40 seconds. Alternatively, you can do a dry shake first (see Working with Eggs, page 30).
3. Strain into a coupe glass.
4. Grate some nutmeg over the top.

MODERN TWIST: *Substitute the brandy with whiskey or aged rum. If you'd like to dial up the richness of this drink, add ¼ ounce of heavy cream and an extra bit of simple syrup, and you've got yourself a dessert!*

EGGNOG

CLASSIC COCKTAILS DONE WELL

SERVES 4 · COUPE

Eggnog is a holiday staple, and a homemade nog made the classic way will taste completely different from anything you'll find at a grocery store. In my experience, even those who claim to dislike eggnog find delight in this version. It takes just ten minutes to whip up a batch that can last you the whole holiday season (if you can hold yourself back from drinking it all!). This recipe is easily doubled or tripled. If you don't have a blender, vigorously shaking the ingredients in a jar will work, but it will be exhausting.

TOOLS

Mixing cup
Measuring cup
Microplane grater
Blender (or jar for shaking)
Bottle or jar with lid
Coupe glasses

INGREDIENTS

4 ounces Cognac
6 ounces milk
2 ounces heavy cream
½ teaspoon freshly grated nutmeg, plus more to serve
2 whole eggs
3 ounces sugar

1. In a mixing cup, combine the Cognac, milk, heavy cream, and grated nutmeg. Set aside.
2. In a blender, mix the eggs on medium-low speed for 30 seconds.
3. Stop the blender, add the sugar, and mix for another 30 seconds.
4. Stop the blender, add the Cognac mixture, and blend for another 30 seconds.
5. Pour into a bottle or jar and chill for at least 2 hours, or overnight.
6. To serve, pour into coupe glasses, and grate nutmeg over the top.

BRANDY

HINT: Although this drink contains raw eggs, the sugar, fat, and alcohol will keep the Eggnog from spoiling. It's a relatively common practice for people to age their Eggnog for months and even years. Over time, the flavors mellow out and the drink becomes even richer. Keep it refrigerated.

HONEYMOON

SERVES 1 · COUPE · FEW INGREDIENTS

The Honeymoon cocktail is a pre-Prohibition drink, first published in 1916. This sweet and tart drink is essentially an apple sour with strong herbal notes. The fruity drink reminds me of an autumn day, and with a name like this, is perfect to celebrate a romantic occasion.

TOOLS	INGREDIENTS
Shaker	1½ ounces apple brandy
Jigger	¾ ounce Bénédictine
Strainer	½ ounce fresh lemon juice
Coupe glass	1 bar spoonful orange liqueur

1. In a shaker, combine the apple brandy, Bénédictine, lemon juice, and orange liqueur, then fill the shaker with ice. Seal and shake for 20 seconds.
2. Strain into a coupe glass.

MODERN TWIST: *Modern interpretations of this drink are much drier, usually calling for a 4:1:1:1 ratio of the four ingredients. This recipe stays truer to the original. Experiment to find your favorite!*

JACK ROSE

SERVES 1 · COUPE · FEW INGREDIENTS

Applejack was a popular spirit in early American history, and the Jack Rose is one of the most well-known cocktails featuring apple brandy. Affirming the drink's popularity in the 1920s, the Jack Rose makes an appearance in Ernest Hemingway's 1926 novel, *The Sun Also Rises*. This drink is fruity, tangy, and a beautiful crimson color that's sure to delight! *SEE PAGE 108 FOR PHOTO.*

TOOLS	INGREDIENTS
Shaker	2 ounces apple brandy
Jigger	¾ ounce fresh lemon juice
Strainer	½ ounce grenadine
Coupe glass	(page 20)

1. In a shaker, combine the apple brandy, lemon juice, and grenadine, then fill the shaker with ice. Seal and shake for 20 seconds.
2. Strain into a coupe glass.

MODERN TWIST: *Grenadine, raspberry syrup, and berry jams can be used interchangeably in this recipe for the fruity component. If using berry jam, use 1 teaspoon of jam accompanied by ¼ ounce of simple syrup or more to taste.*

SIDECAR

SERVES 1 · COUPE · FEW INGREDIENTS

The Sidecar, a true classic, has inspired many riffs throughout cocktail history. It's possible that this early 1900s drink itself is a simplified version of the more elaborate Brandy Crusta (page 113), but alcohol history is often fuzzy, so it's hard to be sure of any origin story. The Sidecar is best recognized by its crunchy sugar rim, and overall is rich and mild, yet spiritous. *SEE PAGE 108 FOR PHOTO.*

TOOLS	INGREDIENTS
Small bowl	Sugar, to rim the glass
Coupe glass	½ ounce fresh lemon juice, plus more for the rim
Shaker	
Jigger	2 ounces Cognac
Strainer	¾ ounce orange liqueur

1. Pour some sugar into a small bowl. Wet the edge of a coupe glass with water or lemon juice. Dip the glass rim into the sugar bowl, then set aside.
2. In a shaker, combine the lemon juice, Cognac, and orange liqueur, then fill the shaker with ice. Seal and shake for 20 seconds.
3. Strain into the prepared coupe glass.

HINT: *The Cognac really defines the Sidecar, so consider using a high-quality, longer-aged Cognac (VSOP/Reserve) for greater depth of flavor.*

CLASSIC COCKTAILS DONE WELL

BRANDY

129

HINT: To get a better understanding of what each base spirit adds to the drink, and find your favorite, try an all-Cognac version, an all-whiskey version, and this 50/50 original!

VIEUX CARRÉ

SERVES 1 · ROCKS GLASS

The Vieux Carré, which means "Old Square," is a New Orleans classic from the historic Hotel Monteleone's Carousel Bar, which is literally a rotating carousel. It's an incredible experience and not to miss if you're ever in New Orleans. This cocktail pays tribute to the diverse ethnic backgrounds of the inhabitants of the old town: rye for the Americans, Cognac and Bénédictine for the French, vermouth for the Italians, and bitters for the Caribbean natives. If you enjoy herbal spirit-forward drinks, give this one a try.

TOOLS
Rocks glass
Mixing glass
Jigger
Bar spoon
Strainer
Cocktail pick

INGREDIENTS
1 ounce Cognac
1 ounce rye whiskey
1 ounce sweet vermouth
¼ ounce Bénédictine
1 dash Angostura aromatic bitters
1 dash Peychaud's bitters
Cocktail cherries, for garnish

1. Fill a rocks glass with ice or one large cube.
2. In a mixing glass, combine the Cognac, whiskey, vermouth, Bénédictine, and both bitters, then fill the mixing glass three-quarters full with ice. Stir for 40 seconds.
3. Strain into the ice-filled rocks glass.
4. Skewer 1 or 2 cocktail cherries on a pick and place it inside the glass.

RUM

Clockwise from top left: Rum Daisy, Hemingway Daiquiri, Grog, Rum Punch

AIR MAIL

SERVES 1 · COUPE

The earliest publication of the Air Mail cocktail can be found in a 1930 Cuban Bacardi pamphlet, and the drink is named for the air mail system which began service in Cuba within that decade. During Prohibition (1920–1933), Americans flocked to Cuba looking for drinks and a good time. The Air Mail is sweet, tart, and bubbly—a refreshing, light sipper. Think of it as a rum version of the French 75 (page 46), or a bubbly version of a Daiquiri (page 141).

TOOLS	INGREDIENTS
Shaker	1½ ounces gold rum
Jigger	½ ounce fresh lime juice
Strainer	½ ounce honey syrup (page 20)
Coupe glass	2 ounces sparkling wine
Bar spoon	Lime slice, for garnish

1. In a shaker, combine the rum, lime juice, and honey syrup, then fill the shaker with ice. Seal and shake for 20 seconds.
2. Strain into a coupe glass.
3. Top with the sparkling wine, give it a brief stir, and place the slice of lime inside the glass.

HINT: *Some gold rums are mild, honeylike, and light, while others are pungent, heavy, and full of deep oak warmth. Cuban rums follow the Spanish style of distillation and are usually lighter in flavor. Choose a Spanish-style rum for something similar in flavor profile.*

BEE'S KISS

SERVES 1 · COUPE · FEW INGREDIENTS

This recipe hails from *Trader Vic's Book of Food & Drink*, originally published in 1946. Victor Bergeron, or Trader Vic, is most well-known for his popular chain of restaurants. Although the theme of his establishments is not culturally accurate, they invented many cocktails inspired by flavors from the Pacific Islands and Asia, including the Mai Tai and this delightful drink. The Bee's Kiss is balanced, creamy, and frankly, quite dangerous. It's light enough to enjoy any time of day, but it makes a killer dessert.

TOOLS
Shaker
Jigger
Strainer
Coupe glass

INGREDIENTS
1½ ounces light rum
¼ ounce honey syrup (page 20)
¼ ounce heavy cream

1. In a shaker, combine the rum, honey syrup, and heavy cream, then fill the shaker with ice. Seal and shake for 20 seconds.
2. Strain into a coupe glass.

MODERN TWIST: *In place of the light rum, try an aged gold rum and sprinkle freshly grated nutmeg over the top for a richer, spicier version. Look for the specific words "Aged 5 years" (or longer) on the label—not just a number.*

BUMBO

SERVES 1 · ROCKS GLASS · FEW INGREDIENTS

The Bumbo is essentially a rum sling and the granddaddy of many rum cocktails. In the olden days, you'd take a swig of rum with some water, and simply add sugar and some spices to make the low-quality liquor more palatable. The modernized take replaces the water with ice but otherwise maintains true to its simplicity.

TOOLS

Rocks glass

Mixing glass

Jigger

Bar spoon

Strainer

Microplane grater

INGREDIENTS

2 ounces gold rum

¼ ounce simple syrup (page 20)

Whole nutmeg, for grating

1. Fill a rocks glass with ice or one large cube.
2. In a mixing glass, combine the rum and simple syrup, then fill the mixing glass three-quarters full with ice. Stir for 40 seconds.
3. Strain into the ice-filled rocks glass.
4. Grate some nutmeg over the top.

MODERN TWIST: *Try swapping the nutmeg for cinnamon, cloves, or allspice.*

DAIQUIRI

CLASSIC COCKTAILS DONE WELL

SERVES 1 · COUPE · FEW INGREDIENTS

The Daiquiri is the one essential rum cocktail to know. Although the term *Daiquiri* is often misapplied to a host of fruity frozen sugary drinks, the classic Daiquiri is nothing more than the magic refreshing trifecta of rum, lime, and sugar. Given its simplicity, it's often regarded as one of the best ways to evaluate a new rum. The base template then opens the doors to many variations—other than changing the rum, you can play around with ratios, try flavored syrups or liqueurs, or muddle in fruits, herbs, and spices.

TOOLS	INGREDIENTS
Shaker	2 ounces rum, any kind
Jigger	¾ ounce fresh lime juice
Strainer	¾ ounce simple syrup
Coupe glass	(page 20)

1. In a shaker, combine the rum, lime juice, and simple syrup, then fill the shaker with ice. Seal and shake for 20 seconds.
2. Strain into a coupe glass.

   HINT: *Before juicing the lime, cut a slice of lime peel and drop it into the shaker to make your Daiquiri even more refreshing. The oils from the peel will add an extra layer of aroma.*

RUM

DOCTOR FUNK

SERVES 1 · ROCKS GLASS

The Doctor Funk is named after Dr. Bernard Funk, a well-known nineteenth-century physician who spent time in the South Pacific. He was known to serve a "medicinal tonic" of lime, absinthe, grenadine, and seltzer. This drink was adopted by American tiki bar pioneers, who added rum to the mix. It was so popular that bars often came up with their own "Doctor __" name for their house version of the drink. Distinguished by the anise flavors from the absinthe, this refreshing drink otherwise resembles a fruity limeade.

TOOLS	INGREDIENTS
Rocks glass	1½ ounces light rum
Shaker	¾ ounce fresh lime juice
Jigger	½ ounce grenadine (page 20)
Strainer	1 bar spoonful absinthe
Bar spoon	1 ounce sparkling water

1. Fill a rocks glass with ice.
2. In a shaker, combine the rum, lime juice, grenadine, and absinthe, then fill the shaker with ice. Seal and shake for 20 seconds.
3. Strain the drink into the ice-filled rocks glass.
4. Top with the sparkling water and give it a brief stir. Serve with a straw.

HINT: *When measuring with a bar spoon, it can be easy to overpour, so do this over your jigger or an extra glass to avoid accidentally adding too much directly into the shaker.*

GROG

SERVES 1 · ROCKS GLASS · FEW INGREDIENTS

Grog was a traditional naval drink composed of rum, lime, and sugar—served at ambient temperature, given that ice was not readily available. In the eighteenth century, the British Royal Navy would receive a daily midday rum ration, which caused quite a drunkenness problem. Admiral Edward "Old Grog" Vernon started enforcing that the rum be watered down, and he offered sailors the option to trade their bread and salt rations for lime and sugar to improve the flavor of the diluted rum. With that, Grog was born and would become a beloved naval drink for centuries. SEE PAGE 132 FOR PHOTO.

TOOLS

Shaker

Jigger

Rocks glass

INGREDIENTS

2 ounces gold rum

½ ounce fresh lime juice

½ ounce simple syrup (page 20)

Lime wedge, for garnish

1. In a shaker, combine the rum, lime juice, and simple syrup, then fill the shaker with ice. Seal and shake for 20 seconds.
2. Pour everything (ice included) into the rocks glass.
3. Place the lime wedge inside the glass.

THROWBACK: *For an old-school Grog, replace the ice with 1 to 2 ounces of water, and use raw brown sugar instead of simple syrup. Skip the shaker and mix everything in the glass.*

HEMINGWAY DAIQUIRI

SHAKEN

CLASSIC COCKTAILS DONE WELL

SERVES 2 · COUPE

The Hemingway Daiquiri is fondly attributed to Ernest Hemingway, who moved to Cuba in the 1930s to focus on his writing and started frequenting the El Floridita bar. The diabetic Hemingway would order his Daiquiri doubly strong and extremely dry. (That's why this recipe serves two.) The original is not the most balanced, so this recipe is adapted for taste. *SEE PAGE 132 FOR PHOTO.*

TOOLS
Shaker
Jigger
Strainer
Coupe glasses

INGREDIENTS
4 ounces light rum
2 ounces fresh grapefruit juice
1 ounce fresh lime juice
½ ounce Luxardo maraschino liqueur
½ ounce simple syrup (page 20)
Lime slice, for garnish

1. In a shaker, combine the rum, grapefruit juice, lime juice, maraschino liqueur, and simple syrup, then fill the shaker with ice. Seal and shake for 20 seconds.
2. Strain into two coupe glasses.
3. Cut a slit halfway through two lime slices and place one on the rim of each glass.

THROWBACK: *To re-create Hemingway's original order, use 4 ounces light rum, 1 ounce fresh lime juice, ½ ounce fresh grapefruit juice, and a bar spoonful of maraschino liqueur. Serve with powdery shaved or blended ice.*

RUM

145

KNICKERBOCKER

SERVES 1 · ROCKS GLASS · FEW INGREDIENTS

The Knickerbocker, dating back to the mid-1800s, is a refreshing fruity drink, brimming with aromatic flavors. The traditional recipe is made using raspberry syrup, but this version uses pomegranate syrup (grenadine) since it's one of our home bar staples.

TOOLS

Shaker
Jigger
Rocks glass

INGREDIENTS

2 ounces gold rum
½ ounce fresh lime juice
¼ ounce grenadine (page 20)
1 bar spoonful orange liqueur
Fresh berries, for garnish (optional)

1. In a shaker, combine the rum, lime juice, grenadine, and orange liqueur, then fill the shaker with ice. Seal and shake for 20 seconds.
2. Pour everything (ice included) into the rocks glass.
3. Top the drink with a handful of fresh berries (if using).

HINT: *If you'd like to try the raspberry version, a quick alternative to prepared raspberry syrup is to muddle five fresh raspberries with ¼ ounce simple syrup (page 20) in your shaker (in place of the grenadine) and shake everything together. To remove the bits of crushed raspberries, strain the drink over fresh ice into your glass.*

HINT: There is a wide spectrum of flavors among light-colored rums. Some clear rums are bright and grassy, while others taste like an overripe fruit salad. For a classic Mojito, choose a mild-flavored rum (Don Q Cristal, Flor de Caña Extra Seco, Cruzan Light Rum), although the Mojito recipe is versatile enough to also work well with other styles.

MOJITO

SERVES 1 · COLLINS GLASS

Like many other rum classics, the Mojito is composed of the holy trinity of rum, lime, and sugar. Popularized in Cuba during American Prohibition, it won the fancy of American travelers. The recipe is very similar to a Tom Collins (page 69) or a Mint Julep (page 93), but the substitution of light rum gives this drink a whole different flavor profile, without any herbal or spiced notes. It's clean, bright, and totally refreshing.

TOOLS

Collins glass
Jigger
Bar spoon
Muddler (optional)

INGREDIENTS

8 to 10 fresh mint leaves, plus more for garnish
¾ ounce simple syrup (page 20)
2 ounces light rum
¾ ounce fresh lime juice, reserving a used lime wedge
2 ounces sparkling water

1. In a collins glass, combine the mint and simple syrup.
2. Use a bar spoon or a muddler to gently bruise the mint leaves without pulverizing them.
3. Add the rum, lime juice, and used lime wedge, and give it a stir.
4. Fill the glass with crushed ice, add the sparkling water, then stir until the ice is integrated.
5. Add a fresh bouquet of mint on top and enjoy with a straw.

QUEEN'S PARK SWIZZLE

CLASSIC COCKTAILS DONE WELL

RUM

SERVES 1 · COLLINS GLASS

The Queen's Park Swizzle is both a beautiful drink and a conversation piece. This early 1900s drink was created and served at the Queen's Park Hotel in Trinidad, the birth country of the famous Angostura aromatic bitters. Trader Vic's later enthusiastic promotion of this drink at his American tiki bars played a big role in its lasting popularity. Though somewhat similar to a Mojito (page 149), this treat is richer in flavor, typically made with a full-flavored gold rum and aromatic bitters.

TOOLS

Collins glass
Jigger
Bar spoon
Muddler (optional)

INGREDIENTS

8 to 10 fresh mint leaves, plus more for garnish
½ ounce simple syrup (page 20)
Lime wedge, for muddling
2 ounces gold rum
½ ounce fresh lime juice
8 to 10 dashes Angostura aromatic bitters

1. In a collins glass, combine the mint, simple syrup, and the lime wedge.
2. Use a bar spoon or muddler to gently bruise the mint leaves without pulverizing them.
3. Add the rum and lime juice and stir.
4. Fill the glass with crushed ice, then stir until the glass is frosty cold.
5. Top off the drink with more crushed ice.
6. Shake the bitters over the top until it forms a nice layer of color.
7. Add a fresh bouquet of mint on top and enjoy with a straw.

HINT: For consistent flavor, mix the bitters into the cocktail before drinking. The layered look is mainly for presentation.

RUM COW

SHAKEN

CLASSIC COCKTAILS DONE WELL

SERVES 1 · COLLINS GLASS

The Rum Cow was created around the late 1930s by Donn "the Beach-comber" Beach, who popularized rum cocktails in America through his nautical-themed bars, inspired by his travels to Oceania. Donn was born in New Orleans, and this drink is an ode to the popular brandy milk punches from the city. As written, the Rum Cow is a light creamy drink. It can be served cold or hot, and can be scaled up to serve a crowd or scaled down for a stronger drink.

TOOLS

Shaker
Jigger
Microplane grater
Collins glass

INGREDIENTS

6 ounces whole milk
2 ounces gold rum
½ ounce simple syrup (page 20)
1 dash Angostura aromatic bitters
Whole nutmeg, for grating

1. In a shaker, combine the milk, rum, simple syrup, bitters, and a bit of freshly grated nutmeg, then fill the shaker with ice. Seal and shake for 20 seconds.
2. Pour everything (ice included) into the collins glass.

HINT: *To scale up as a punch, increase the milk to 8 ounces per serving, then multiply all ingredients by the number of servings needed. To scale down for a stronger drink, decrease the milk to 3 ounces. For a hot version, heat the milk, then stir together all the ingredients.*

RUM

153

RUM DAISY

SERVES 1 · ROCKS GLASS · FEW INGREDIENTS

This simple three-ingredient drink from *Trader Vic's Book of Food & Drink* is refreshing and fruity. Just like the Gin Daisy (page 54) and Tequila-based Margarita "Daisy" (page 171), the Rum Daisy follows the same template of a spirit, citrus, and fruit liqueur. Perfect for a warm day or to kick off your evening happy hour! *SEE PAGE 132 FOR PHOTO.*

TOOLS
Shaker
Jigger
Rocks glass

INGREDIENTS
2 ounces light rum
½ ounce fresh lime juice, reserving a used lime wedge
¼ ounce grenadine (page 20)

1. In a shaker, combine the rum, lime juice, used lime wedge, and grenadine, then fill the shaker with ice. Seal and shake for 20 seconds.
2. Pour everything (ice included) into the rocks glass.

MODERN TWIST: *Try using a gold rum for a richer drink. Jamaican rums have strong tropical fruit notes and work extremely well in this drink. If using a fuller-flavored rum, increase the grenadine to ½ ounce to balance the flavor. A sprig of mint to garnish the drink adds a wonderful fresh accent.*

RUM PUNCH

SERVES 8 · SMALL GLASSES

The Rum Punch is enjoyed on many Caribbean islands and perfect for parties. There is even a rhyme for the recipe: "One of sour, two of sweet, three of strong, and four of weak." Lime is the sour, sugar is the sweet, rum is the strong, and water or ice is the weak. Don't forget to add a bit of spice to make things nice! *SEE PAGE 132 FOR PHOTO.*

TOOLS	INGREDIENTS
Punch bowl	5 ounces fresh lime juice
Measuring cup	10 ounces simple syrup (page 20)
Jigger	15 ounces gold rum
Microplane grater	15 ounces water
Bar spoon	½ ounce Angostura aromatic bitters
Small glasses	1 teaspoon freshly grated nutmeg

1. In a punch bowl, combine the lime juice, simple syrup, rum, water, bitters, and nutmeg and stir to combine.
2. If possible, refrigerate for 2 to 3 hours to allow the flavors to come together.
3. When ready to serve, fill your punch bowl with large ice cubes. Adjust for taste as needed. The drink will dilute over time, so consider starting a bit on the stronger side.
4. Serve in small glasses with ice.

MODERN TWIST: *Fancy up your punch with fresh orange or grapefruit juices, alternatively substitute a portion of the simple syrup with honey syrup (page 20) or grenadine (page 20).*

OTHER SPIRITS & LIQUEURS

Clockwise from top left: Rosita, Paloma, Margarita, Long Island Iced Tea

AMERICANO

SERVES 1 · COLLINS GLASS · FEW INGREDIENTS

This refreshingly bitter aperitivo is typically enjoyed before a meal to stimulate the appetite. The Americano is based on a popular mid-1800s Italian drink called the Milano-Torino, which contained just Campari and sweet vermouth. During American Prohibition, this variant of the Milano-Torino became popular among American tourists and so was called the Americano. It's a low-ABV (alcohol by volume) treat—delightfully flavorful and simple to make.

TOOLS

Collins glass

Jigger

Bar spoon

INGREDIENTS

1½ ounces Campari

1½ ounces sweet vermouth

4 ounces sparkling water

½ slice of orange

1. Fill a collins glass with ice.
2. Add the Campari and sweet vermouth, then top with the sparkling water.
3. Give everything a quick stir and place the orange slice inside the glass.

THROWBACK: *For something a bit heavier, try the original Milano-Torino cocktail—just omit the sparkling water. Stir the Campari and sweet vermouth with the ice, then strain over fresh ice in a rocks glass and serve with an orange slice.*

CHAMPAGNE COCKTAIL

CLASSIC COCKTAILS DONE WELL

SERVES 1 · CHAMPAGNE FLUTE · FEW INGREDIENTS

The original drink referred to as a "Cocktail" was nothing more than a slightly sweetened spirit with a bit of water and spice. These days, the whiskey-based Cocktail is widely known as an Old Fashioned (page 94), but the Champagne version of the Cocktail is less talked about. This makes a fantastic brunch cocktail, and the sugar cube adds fizzy pizzazz! Use a quality sparkling wine you'd enjoy drinking on its own. For more depth and complexity, add a small splash of Cognac.

TOOLS
Small bowl
Jigger
Champagne flute
Peeler

INGREDIENTS
1 sugar cube (see Hint)
4 to 6 dashes Angostura aromatic bitters
5 ounces sparkling wine
Lemon peel, for garnish

1. Place the sugar cube inside a small bowl and dash it with the bitters until it's soaked.
2. Pour the sparkling wine into a Champagne flute.
3. Drop the bitters-soaked sugar cube into the wine and watch it fizz!
4. Express the oils from the lemon peel over the top of the drink, rub the peel along the rim of the glass, then drop the peel into the drink.

HINT: *If you don't have sugar cubes, substitute ½ ounce simple syrup (page 20). Just add the syrup and bitters directly into the wine-filled glass and stir.*

OTHER SPIRITS & LIQUEURS

CHRYSANTHEMUM

SERVES 1 · COUPE · FEW INGREDIENTS

This early 1900s drink features a deep herbal richness that's aromatic yet mild. The Chrysanthemum is perfect both for winding down and starting out your night; given its lower alcohol content, it's great for enjoying during the day as well. Don't be deceived—while this cocktail is light on ABV (alcohol by volume), it's still massive on flavor.

TOOLS	INGREDIENTS
Mixing glass	2 ounces dry vermouth
Jigger	½ ounce Bénédictine
Bar spoon	1 bar spoonful absinthe
Strainer	Orange peel, for garnish
Coupe glass	
Peeler	

1. In a mixing glass, combine the vermouth, Bénédictine, and absinthe, then fill the glass three-quarters full with ice. Stir for 40 seconds.
2. Strain into a coupe glass.
3. Express the oils from the orange peel over the top of the drink, rub the peel along the rim of the glass, then drop the peel into the drink.

   HINT: *Dry vermouth has a short lifespan once opened (a couple months if refrigerated), so it's usually best to buy the smallest bottle you can find. Old vermouth will taste very different and unpleasant.*

GARIBALDI

CLASSIC COCKTAILS DONE WELL

SERVES 1 · ROCKS GLASS · FEW INGREDIENTS

This classic Italian cocktail makes a perfect brunch drink. This refreshingly bitter delight is very simple with just two ingredients, and the process makes all the difference. Most important, freshly squeezed orange juice is a must. Store-bought juices undergo significant preservation processing, which completely changes the flavors. Secondly, you'll want to froth and aerate the orange juice, preferably with a blender.

TOOLS

Blender, milk frother, or jar with lid

Rocks glass

Jigger

Bar spoon

INGREDIENTS

4 ounces fresh orange juice

1½ ounces Campari

1 orange wedge

1. Pour the orange juice into a blender and give it a few whirls until lighter in color. You can also use a milk frother or add the orange juice to a jar and shake it fervently to create aeration and bubbles.
2. Fill a rocks glass with ice, then add the Campari.
3. Add the aerated orange juice and stir.
4. Perch the orange wedge across the top of the glass for garnish.

HINT: *To batch for a crowd, multiply the recipe by the number of servings and serve in a pitcher or bowl with plenty of ice.*

OTHER SPIRITS & LIQUEURS

KAMIKAZE

SERVES 1 · COUPE

The Kamikaze was a defining cocktail during the vodka revolution in the 1970s. The original recipe included just vodka, Triple Sec, and lime juice, often in equal proportions, and this combination leaves something to be desired. The following recipe addresses the original's shortcomings by adding a bit of simple syrup as well as an entire wedge of lime to infuse some aromatic oils into the drink.

TOOLS

Shaker
Jigger
Strainer
Coupe glass

INGREDIENTS

1½ ounces vodka
¾ ounce orange liqueur
¾ ounce fresh lime juice
¼ ounce simple syrup (page 20)
1 lime wedge and 1 slice of lime

1. In a shaker, combine the vodka, orange liqueur, lime juice, simple syrup, and the lime wedge, then fill the shaker with ice. Seal and shake for 20 seconds.
2. Strain into a coupe glass and gently float the slice of lime on top.

MODERN TWIST: *The famous Cosmopolitan is a riff on the Kamikaze, with the simple addition of a splash (1 ounce) of cranberry juice. Unsweetened cranberry juice has the purest flavor, but since it's quite tart, add a bit more simple syrup and reduce some of the lime juice to compensate.*

CLASSIC COCKTAILS DONE WELL

OTHER SPIRITS & LIQUEURS

LEMON DROP

SERVES 1 · COUPE

Although sometimes served in shot form, the classic Lemon Drop is effectively a vodka variation of the brandy-based Sidecar (page 129). Invented in the 1970s in San Francisco, this drink was designed to attract female clientele to a singles bar. Simple in taste, this refreshing drink is clean and easy to enjoy.

TOOLS

Small bowl

Coupe glass

Shaker

Jigger

Strainer

INGREDIENTS

Sugar, to rim the glass

¾ ounce fresh lemon juice, plus more for the rim

1½ ounces vodka

½ ounce orange liqueur

½ ounce simple syrup (page 20)

1. Pour some sugar into a small bowl. Wet the edge of a coupe glass with water or lemon juice. Dip the glass rim into the sugar bowl, then set aside.

2. In a shaker, combine the vodka, lemon juice, orange liqueur, and simple syrup, then fill the shaker with ice. Seal and shake for 20 seconds.

3. Strain into the prepared coupe glass.

HINT: *Sugar and salt rims are common in sour-style drinks, which means you should already have a piece of cut citrus handy. For convenience (and flavor!), just use the citrus juice to wet your glass for the rim.*

LONG ISLAND ICED TEA

SERVES 1 · COLLINS GLASS

This recipe requires a few more ingredients than most others in this book, but this famous classic deserves a mention. Named for its visual resemblance to iced tea, this sweet and tart sipper is ready for a fun night. *SEE PAGE 156 FOR PHOTO.*

TOOLS

Shaker
Jigger
Collins glass
Strainer
Bar spoon

INGREDIENTS

½ ounce gin
½ ounce light rum
½ ounce vodka
½ ounce Tequila
½ ounce orange liqueur
¾ ounce fresh lemon juice
¾ ounce simple syrup (page 20)
2 ounces cola
Lemon slice, for garnish

1. In a shaker, combine the gin, rum, vodka, Tequila, orange liqueur, lemon juice, and simple syrup, then fill the shaker with ice. Seal and shake for 20 seconds.
2. Fill a collins glass with fresh ice, then strain the drink into the glass.
3. Top with the cola and give it a brief stir.
4. Place the lemon slice inside the glass and serve with a straw.

HINT: *Scale up for a party simply by multiplying all ingredients by the number of servings, and mix them together in a punch bowl or drink dispenser. Add plenty of ice for proper dilution.*

CLASSIC COCKTAILS DONE WELL

OTHER SPIRITS & LIQUEURS

MARGARITA

SERVES 1 · ROCKS GLASS

The Margarita was likely popularized around the early twentieth century. The frozen version of the Margarita emerged in the 1950s, and its popularity boomed with the invention of the frozen Margarita machine. Make the frozen version by mixing the ingredients with a cup of ice in a high-speed blender. *SEE PAGE 156 FOR PHOTO.*

TOOLS

Small bowl
Rocks glass
Shaker
Jigger

INGREDIENTS

Salt, to rim the glass
¾ ounce fresh lime juice, plus more for the rim
2 ounces Tequila
¾ ounce orange liqueur
¼ ounce simple syrup (page 20)
Lime wedge, for garnish

1. Pour some salt into a small bowl. Wet the edge of a rocks glass with water or lime juice. Dip the glass rim into the salt bowl, then set aside.
2. In a shaker, combine the lime juice, Tequila, orange liqueur, and simple syrup, then fill the shaker with ice. Seal and shake for 20 seconds.
3. Pour everything (ice included) into the prepared rocks glass.
4. Drop the lime wedge into the glass.

MODERN TWIST: *To make a Tommy's Margarita, replace the liqueur and simple syrup with ½ ounce total of agave nectar. Or try muddling in some fresh fruit or spicy peppers!*

MOSCOW MULE

SERVES 1 · ROCKS GLASS · FEW INGREDIENTS

According to legend, in a series of coincidences, a struggling vodka salesman met a ginger beer supplier and a copper mug factory heiress, and the three joined forces to create the Copper Mug Moscow Mule. This clean, refreshing, and slightly spicy drink was heavily marketed and gained popularity in Hollywood, then spread across America. You can enjoy this drink in a rocks glass, but if you end up making it often, consider getting some copper mugs for added coolness—copper's thermal conductivity will make your drink feel extra cold.

TOOLS
Rocks glass
Jigger
Bar spoon

INGREDIENTS
2 ounces vodka
½ ounce fresh lime juice
4 ounces ginger beer
Lime wedge, for garnish

1. Fill a rocks glass with ice.
2. Add the vodka and lime juice, then top with the ginger beer. Give it a quick stir to combine.
3. Add the lime wedge and serve with a straw.

MODERN TWIST: *For added freshness, top your cocktail with a sprig of mint. You can also gently muddle it in the glass as the first step.*

NEGRONI SBAGLIATO

CLASSIC COCKTAILS DONE WELL

OTHER SPIRITS & LIQUEURS

SERVES 1 · CHAMPAGNE FLUTE · FEW INGREDIENTS

Sbagliato is a fun word, which translates to "mistake" in Italian, so this drink is called a "Mistaken Negroni." This aperitivo-style drink dates back to the 1960s, and the story goes that it was invented when a bartender mistakenly served a Negroni (page 65) with Prosecco instead of gin. A perfect drink for brunch or pre-dinner, the Negroni Sbagliato has a bittersweet flavor that opens up the appetite. It's similar to the Americano (page 159), but with a bit more bite given the use of sparkling wine.

TOOLS

Champagne flute
Jigger
Bar spoon

INGREDIENTS

1 ounce Campari
1 ounce sweet vermouth
2 ounces sparkling wine
(preferably Prosecco)
½ slice of orange

1. Fill a Champagne flute with ice.
2. Add the Campari and sweet vermouth, then top with the sparkling wine.
3. Give everything a quick stir and place the orange slice inside the glass.

HINT: *In case you ever need to say this out loud, sbagliato is roughly pronounced sba-ya-toe. The Italian "gli" sounds similar to an English "y" or Spanish "ll."*

PALOMA

SERVES 1 · COLLINS GLASS

This classic drink is perfect for warm days. The Paloma has been enjoyed in Mexico since at least the mid-twentieth century. Often made using just Tequila and Squirt grapefruit soda, this version is a little bit fancier. *SEE PAGE 156 FOR PHOTO.*

TOOLS

Small bowl

Collins glass

Shaker

Jigger

Strainer

Bar spoon

INGREDIENTS

Salt, to rim the glass

¾ ounce fresh lime juice, plus more for the rim

2 ounces Tequila

1½ ounces fresh grapefruit juice

1 ounce simple syrup (page 20)

2 ounces sparkling water

½ slice of grapefruit

1. Pour some salt in a small bowl. Wet the edge of a collins glass with water or lime juice. Dip the glass rim into the salt bowl, then carefully fill the salt-rimmed glass with ice.
2. In a shaker, combine the Tequila, grapefruit juice, lime juice, and simple syrup, then fill the shaker with ice. Seal and shake for 20 seconds.
3. Strain into the prepared collins glass. Add the sparkling water and give it a stir to combine.
4. Slit the grapefruit slice halfway and place on the rim of the glass.

THROWBACK: *To make this with soda, build the drink over ice in the collins glass with one part Tequila, two parts grapefruit soda, and a squeeze of lime juice.*

CLASSIC COCKTAILS DONE WELL

OTHER SPIRITS & LIQUEURS

ROSITA

SERVES 1 · ROCKS GLASS

This cocktail steps away from the sweet-and-tart realm common for Tequila drinks and into bitter and herbal territory. First documented in the 1970s cocktail book *Mr. Boston Official Bartender's Guide*, it was reintroduced by cocktail legend Gary "Gaz" Regan in the 1990s.

SEE PAGE 156 FOR PHOTO.

TOOLS

Rocks glass
Mixing glass
Jigger
Bar spoon
Strainer
Peeler

INGREDIENTS

1½ ounces Tequila (preferably reposado)

½ ounce dry vermouth

½ ounce sweet vermouth

½ ounce Campari

1 dash Angostura aromatic bitters

Lemon peel, for garnish

1. Fill a rocks glass with ice or one large cube.
2. In a mixing glass, combine the Tequila, dry and sweet vermouths, Campari, and bitters, then fill the glass three-quarters full with ice. Stir for 40 seconds.
3. Strain into the ice-filled rocks glass.
4. Express the oils from the lemon peel over the top of the drink, rub the peel along the rim of the glass, then drop the peel into the drink.

MODERN TWIST: *Consider infusing either the Tequila or Campari with strawberries to use in this recipe. Fill a jar with sliced strawberries and cover with the alcohol. After a few days, strain out the strawberries. This will keep refrigerated for at least two to three months.*

CLASSIC COCKTAILS DONE WELL

OTHER SPIRITS & LIQUEURS

ACKNOWLEDGMENTS

T hank you to my husband, Dylan, for supporting me throughout the entirety of this project, and through all the cocktail projects in our household over the years. Thank you for allowing us to literally build a home bar in our apartment (then condo, then house), for your never-ending support, and most directly, for the months of cocktail tastings of numerous variations of each drink in this book.

Thank you to all my wonderful friends who helped with this project through cocktail tastings and experiments: Karen, Mee, Logan, Darcy, Tom, Tommy, Brian, Tesla, Maya, and Ankush. All your awesome feedback helped shape the recipes in this book!

Finally, this hobby would not be anywhere nearly as fulfilling without the incredible Instagram community and friendships I've made, both virtually and in person. The "Drinkstagram" community has nurtured my hobby and driven me to continuously learn more about the history, culture, and artistry of cocktails.

RESOURCES

AUTHOR'S SITES

WEBSITE: barfaith.com

INSTAGRAM: instagram.com/barfaith

YOUTUBE: youtube.com/barfaith

FACEBOOK: facebook.com/BarFaithDrinks

COCKTAIL HISTORY

Wondrich, David. *Imbibe!* New York: Penguin Random House, 2007.

Wondrich, David. *Punch.* New York: Penguin Random House, 2010.

TECHNIQUE AND SETUP

Morgenthaler, Jeffrey. *The Bar Book.* San Francisco: Chronicle Books, 2014.

Day, Alex, Nick Fauchald, and David Kaplan. *Cocktail Codex.* Berkeley, CA: Ten Speed Press, 2014.

Day, Alex, Nick Fauchald, and David Kaplan. *Death & Co: Welcome Home.* Berkeley, CA: Ten Speed Press, 2021.

COCKTAIL RECIPES

Meehan, Jim. *The PDT Cocktail Book.* New York: Sterling Epicure, 2011.

Petraske, Sasha and Georgette Moger-Petraske. *Regarding Cocktails.* New York: Phaidon Press, 2016.

PDT Cocktails iOS app: Digital app version of the recipes in *The PDT Cocktail Book.* mixologytech.com/pdt/index.html

Difford's Guide: Vast online inventory of modern and classic cocktail recipes. diffordsguide.com

Martin's Index iOS app: Thousands of classic cocktails from historical publications. mixologytech.com/martinsindex

RUM RECIPES AND KNOWLEDGE

Berry, Jeff. *Beachbum Berry's Potions of the Caribbean.* New York: Cocktail Kingdom, 2013.

Berry, Jeff. *Beachbum Berry's Sippin' Safari.* San Jose, CA: SLG Publishing, 2007.

Cate, Martin and Rebecca. *Smuggler's Cove.* Berkeley, CA: Ten Speed Press, 2016.

Beachbum Berry's Total Tiki iOS app: Classic American tiki cocktail recipes aggregated by tiki historian Jeff Berry. mixologytech.com/totaltiki/index.html

Cocktail Wonk's entry on rum: An excellent website full of information about rum, from the basics to a deep dive into its science and history. cocktailwonk.com/all-about-rum

SHOPPING

Cocktail Kingdom: Industry-popular cocktail tools and glassware. cocktailkingdom.com

Crate & Barrel/CB2: Good resources for diverse modern glassware. crateandbarrel.com cb2.com

Wine-searcher: Search engine for regional shops for hard-to-find bottles. wine-searcher.com

COCKTAILS BY OCCASION

BRUNCH
Americano (page 159)
Champagne Cocktail (page 160)
Chrysanthemum (page 163)
French 75 (page 46)
Garibaldi (page 164)
Irish Coffee (page 86)
Negroni Sbagliato (page 174)
Seelbach (page 101)

CLASSIC COCKTAIL PARTY
Daiquiri (page 141)
Manhattan (page 90)
Martini (page 63)
Negroni (page 65)
Old Fashioned (page 94)
Sidecar (page 129)
Tom Collins (page 69)
Whiskey Sour (page 107)

DATE NIGHT
Brandy Crusta (page 113)
Champagne Cocktail (page 160)
Clover Club (page 45)
Honeymoon (page 126)
Jack Rose (page 128)
Pink Lady (page 66)

DAYTIME BARBECUE
Brandy Punch (page 118)
Gin Buck (page 53)

Gold Rush (page 81)
Margarita (page 171)
Moscow Mule (page 173)
Paloma (page 176)
Rum Punch (page 155)
Whiskey Sour (page 107)

SUMMER QUENCHERS
Doctor Funk (page 143)
Gin & Tonic (page 50)
Gin Buck (page 53)
Mint Julep (page 93)
Mojito (page 149)
Moscow Mule (page 173)
Paloma (page 176)
Queen's Park Swizzle (page 150)

MARDI GRAS
Brandy Crusta (page 113)
De La Louisiane (page 80)
Rum Cow (page 153)
Sazerac (page 98)
Vieux Carré (page 131)

WINTER WARMERS
Apple Toddy (page 110)
Eggnog (page 124)
Hot Whiskey Punch (page 82)

INDEX

Page numbers in *italics* indicate photographs.

189

ABOUT THE AUTHOR

FAITH HINGEY is a spirits and cocktail enthusiast in the San Francisco Bay Area. She aspires to demystify the world of craft cocktails and make it an approachable creative indulgence for everyone to enjoy at home. She shares education-focused content about spirits and cocktails on Instagram at @barfaith and on barfaith.com. In her free time outside of cocktails, she enjoys indoor and outdoor gardening, building DIY home projects, and cooking internationally inspired meals.

Copyright © 2022 by Penguin Random House LLC

Published in the United States by Zeitgeist, an imprint of Zeitgeist™,
a division of Penguin Random House LLC, New York.
penguinrandomhouse.com

Zeitgeist™ is a trademark of Penguin Random House LLC

ISBN: 9780593435946
Ebook ISBN: 9780593435731

Photography by Clare Barboza
Styling by Gretchen Rude
Book design by Katy Brown
Edited by Meg Ilasco and Ada Fung

Printed in China

3 5 7 9 10 8 6 4 2

First Edition

VOLUME EQUIVALENTS

Ounces	Milliliters
¼ ounce	7 milliliters
½ ounce	15 milliliters
¾ ounce	21 milliliters
1 ounce	30 milliliters
1½ ounces	45 milliliters
2 ounces	59 milliliters
3 ounces	89 milliliters
4 ounces	118 milliliters
5 ounces	148 milliliters
10 ounces	296 milliliters
15 ounces	444 milliliters
16 ounces	473 milliliters